vivah

design a perfect hindu wedding

meenal atul pandya

Published by:
MeeRa Publications
P.O.Box 812129
Wellesley, MA 02482 0014
781 235 7441
www.MeeraPublications.com

Printed in Hong Kong

ISBN 0-9635539-2-5

Library of Congress Catalog Card Number 99-93353

Book Design by:
Signature Design

First Edition

If you wish to distribute the vedic ceremony part of this book to your guests at your wedding, please contact MeeRa Publications for special rate for bulk purchase.

With Love To

Seema and Haril

whose wedding inspired this book

वक्रतुंड महाकाय सूर्यॅकोटि सम प्रभ
निर्विघ्नम् कुरुमे देव शुभ कार्येषु सर्वदा

Vakratunda mahakay suryakoti sama prabha
Nirvighnam kurume deva shubha karyeshu sarvada

This book is created to help you design the wedding of
your dreams. We are confident that this book will guide
you through the planning process, inspire you to strive for
the best, provide you with a list of resources, and, most
importantly, help you understand the high ideals of the
Hindu marriage ceremony. So use this book and add your
own style to create a perfect wedding - YOUR wedding.

For You Two

The Love that you carry today for each other,

May it grow into respect with each passing year.

The Dreams that you share today with each other,

May they become reality with each passing moment.

The Honesty that you bring today to each other,

May that mature into trust with each passing day.

The Openness that you admire today in each other,

May that help you both become your very best.

The happiness that you feel today being with each other,

May that radiate in everything you do all your life,

As you both share a long life filled with

Health, Wealth and Prosperity.

Acknowledgements

It has been said that you need a village to raise a child. I think similarly it should be said that you need a community to write any book, especially a book of this kind. I have been extremely fortunate to have a large group of friends and family members who helped me with the creation of this book. This book could not have been written without the help of all of you who gave your time, shared your knowledge, and offered your insightful and valuable comments every step of the way. First and foremost, I want to thank Seema and Haril Pandya without whom this book would not have been possible. From conceiving the idea to the final design they both have been extremely vital and important contributors to this book. I want to thank Dr. Mahesh Mehta for offering his insightful comments and suggestions - especially in the understanding of the significance of saptapadi in today's context. His vast knowledge of Hindu religion and customs has benefited this book trememdously. I also want to thank Shri Suryakant Parikh for sharing his knowledge of sanskrit literature and Hindu religion.

Special thanks to Shri Bansi Pandit, whose words of wisdom grace the book and to Shri K.K.Shastri and Swami Shri Tadatmanandji for offering their valuable suggestions. Lots of information and many pictures were provided by many friends and I want to thank them all. Thanks to Anu Radhakrishnan, Gaurang Vaishnav, Banani Datta, Ami Bhatt-Potter, Jayant Sane, Yogesh Patel, and Harihar Joshi for providing information. Many thanks to Nalini Goyal, Amrita Udeshi, Viraj Parikh, Asit Pandya, Renuka Shah, Atul Patel, Ramnik Singh, Satyaja and Harjasjit Singh Bedi and Santosh and Dnyanada Karandikar for sharing their pictures and art work. Last but not the least, I want to thank my husband, Atul, and my daughters Shirali and Amoli for providing their unflinching support, patience and confidence in me to write the book. Their enthusiasm and help has made this project a worthwhile effort for me.

Thank you all.

c o n t

e   n   t   s

Before
We Begin

कोंदात्
कस्मादात्
कामायादात्
कामो दाता
कामः प्रतिग्रहीता
कामः समुद्रमाविशत्
कामेन त्वा प्रतिग्रहएामि
कामैतत्ते
यर्जु वेद

Foreword

Vedas, the treasury of the ancient spiritual and cultural wisdom of India, view creation as a play of consciousness. In this divine play, cosmic consciousness – the creative source of both physical and spiritual phenomena – continuously evolves from lower to higher states of manifestation, and, ultimately, to its unmanifested state of eternal peace and bliss.

The role of humans in this divine play is to evolve from ignorance to knowledge (*tamaso maa jyotir gamaya*) and expand individual consciousness to embrace universal consciousness. For an individual, the purpose of life is thus to realize itself. In other words, our purpose is to realize our own intrinsic nature, which is potentially divine and pure. This self-realization occurs when we free ourselves from the limitations of physical phenomena by working out our past *karma* in accordance with *dharma* (righteousness). The purpose of marriage is to create intelligent progeny to attain realization of the Supreme. For this very reason, marriage is viewed as a *samskara* (sacrament) in the Hindu tradition.

The elaborate ceremonies and the chanting of **mantras** (sacred verses) associated with a typical Hindu marriage are performed strictly in accordance with the Vedic scriptures. To ensure growth and harmony, Vedas divide human life into four *ashrams* our stages:

studentship (*brahmacharya ashram*); householder (*grahastha ashram*); retirement (*vanprastha ashram*); and self-realization (*sanyas ashram*).

At the conclusion of the studentship stage, the marriage *samskara* allows an individual to enter the householder stage, which also forms the foundation for the remaining two stages of human life. Thus, the happiness, peace and prosperity of three-quarters of human life depend upon the success of *grahastha ashram*.

In Hinduism, marriage is not an experiment to investigate whether or not we like our partner. Rather, it is an irrevocable commitment to a lifetime relationship of one-wife-one-husband. In order to satisfy such a commitment, we must be ready, willing and able to subordinate our individual interests and inclinations to the larger ideal of reflecting divine love through lifelong companionship. Hindu philosophy recognizes that there are natural differences in the tastes and tempers, ideals and interests of individuals. The Hindu ideal of marriage is to reconcile these differences to promote a harmonious life. The sacredness of Hindu marriage is reflected in the fact that most of the manifestations of the Ultimate Reality take the form of wedded gods and goddesses in Hinduism.

This book provides a much-needed resource for planning and performing a Hindu marriage ceremony, with a full understanding of the significance of the steps and ceremonies involved. The author has done an excellent job of discussing the social, religious, and cultural dimensions, as well as the practical considerations relative to the institution of marriage in the Hindu tradition.

I believe that this book will greatly help future brides and grooms to strengthen their union and make marriage a wonderful lifelong experience.

Bansi Pandit

Author of *The Hindu Mind*

समानी व आकृतिः
समाना हृदयानि वः
समानमस्तु वो मनो
यथा वः सुसहासति ।।
रिग वेद

Prologue

Marriage is one of the most celebrated aspects of any society. It is also the single most important undertaking of an individual – one that lasts a lifetime (or even longer, according to Hindu philosophy). It touches more lives than almost any other activity we may undertake, and usually plays a key role in the future growth of an individual.

A happy marriage does not come easily. It requires constant nourishment from both partners, particularly as we grow and our responsibilities change. A happy marriage can turn a home into heaven but an unhappy one can turn it into a hell. A lot – more than we realize – depends upon the kind of partner we choose. So much is at stake – our physical and emotional well-being, our mental growth, and our family's happiness. It is also important to remember that marriage is a union and much depends upon the kind of partner we are, and what we offer to the relationship.

The Hindu view of marriage is beyond personal satisfaction. It is a path to your *dharma* (duty), the *dharma* toward your spouse, your children, your parents, your community, and, ultimately, the greater society.

Just as a healthy body is not merely an absence of sickness, a happy marriage is not simply one without obvious conflict.

Once, when I was conducting a workshop for boys and girls in their teens, I asked them if they knew any married couples they thought were happily married.

A boy raised his hand and told of his uncle and aunt in India whose marriage, he said, was very happy. When I asked him why, he said it was because he never saw them fight.

The truth is that we often think a happy marriage is a marriage without conflict. However, a successful marriage is more than that. It is a sense of overall happiness generated from within by loving someone; it is knowing that you can depend on your spouse in any situation; it is the feeling that you are always understood; it is the knowledge that your contribution to the family is respected, quite apart from its monetary value. It is as much about giving as getting. That is why Hindus believe that a good marriage begins with a ceremony that is uplifting, family oriented and harmonious.

As you embark upon this important journey, may God bless you with eternal love, happiness, and inner strength to bring the best to newly created partnership.

Decorative Wedding Entrance

8

May Mitra, Varuna and Aryman grant us freedom and
space enough for us and for our children! May we find
pleasant pathways, good to travel!
Preserve us ever more,
O Gods, with blessings!

Rig Veda

About This Book

Congratulations! You are about to embark upon the most important journey of your life and we are glad to be a part of that journey. This book is written not only to help you with the best possible wedding preparations, but also to help you think beyond the immediate, and to chart the course of your lives toward growth and harmony. This book, we hope, will be your guide, a calendar, a true friend and a marriage counselor all in one. We know that you will need all of these things at some point during the coming year as you go through the ups and downs of the planning for a wedding.

Rituals and Ceremonies:

First and foremost, this book will help you understand some of the most significant and intricate aspects of the ceremony that you will perform with the help of your priest.

We feel that, in order for you to enjoy and appreciate the significance of the *mantras* and the rituals, you need to have some understanding of what happens during the ceremony.

Vedic ceremonies have been around since time immemorial, and have been performed by Hindus all around the world. They have evolved and changed to fit the needs of time and place, yet have retained the very essence of the meanings and emotions. The most beautiful aspect of these ceremonies is that they are designed for your social, emotional, and spiritual growth. A Hindu marriage is a *samskara*, a sacrament, that formulates your new role in life.

With the help of this book, you will participate in the ceremony with perspective and understanding – trademarks of Hinduism – so that you can fully benefit from the rich beauty of the Vedic ceremony.

Regional customs and rituals:

While the fundamental aspects of the ceremonies – such as *saptapadi* and *kanyadaan* – are similar in every wedding ceremony, each region, caste, and sub-caste has evolved its own customs. For example, a Punjabi wedding may be very different from a Tamil wedding, yet both share the core aspects of a Vedic ceremony.

We have tried to include some of the particular characteristics of various states, from Tamilnadu to Punjab and from Gujarat to Bengal. We have also included Jain and Sikh weddings, since they are essentially offshoots of Hinduism, and share many of the central values.

Planning Guide:

Perhaps the most useful part of this book is the Planning Guide where we provide a tried, tested, and dependable step-by-step guide, so you stay in control of the planning process. This work is created from the experiences of several couples and their parents, collected so that you can enjoy the process and feel empowered instead of overwhelmed.

Putting together a large event like a wedding is far from easy. There are a multitude of emotions involved. Two families and their traditions need to be considered, as do your own ideas of an ideal wedding and those of your partner. Indeed, planning your wedding is probably one of the most challenging things you will ever undertake.

So use this book. Read it through first so that you have a clear idea of what is in it. Take notes. Discuss with your partner what fits into your plans to create a memorable experience, not just for you, but also for your guests.

Tips and Suggestions:

Throughout this book, you will find tips for a successful wedding and a happy married life. They are the culmination of experience and expertise. We have collected these "words of wisdom" from writers, thinkers, religious leaders, and newly-weds themselves.

Your New Relations:

Marriage creates a whole new set of relationships and a brand new family for both of you. Since a Hindu wedding is about families, we have provided information on these new relations, what they are called, each one's Sanskrit and Hindi titles, and how you are related to different individuals in your spouse's family.

It is interesting to note that each relationship has a specific name. Perhaps this is an indication of how developed Hindu family system has been for thousands of years.

Resources:

Above all, we have provided a list of resources in your area, from *mehndi* (henna) artists to hall decorators. Our list of selected wedding service providers will help you identify and find every service you will need. We also give you sample items that you can use for your own wedding. For example, in some parts of India, a special recitation is made for the couple. It is called *manglashtak* and is often written especially for them. We have provided a sample *manglashtak* in Sanskrit and Gujarati to use if you wish. We have also provided a glossary of all the words used in italics.

This book is written with you and your big day in mind. We want you to have the best possible wedding and to experience a happy and uplifting married life.

We hope that our book helps you enjoy the planning process, your wedding day, and most importantly, the rest of your life together.

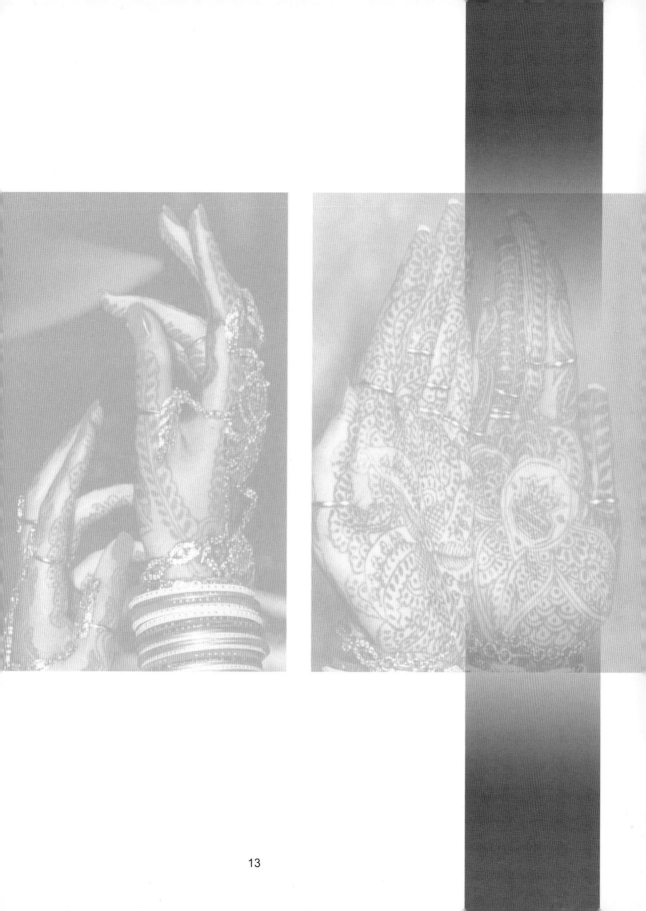

Vedic Ceremony

The word "samskara" also refers to "value" so the important sixteen samskaras together help inculcate values that Hindus have traditionally cherished. Interestingly, the word "samskruti" which means culture is derived from the word samskara.

What is a Hindu Marriage?

Hindu Marriage is a Samskara

Since the dawn of civilization, marriage ceremonies and rituals have reflected the most celebrated values of each culture. Hindu culture celebrates marriage as a *samskara*, a sacrament, a rite of passage in which two individuals start their journey into the *grahastha aashram*.

By making marriage a sacrament, Hindus have elevated the physical union of two individuals to the spiritual. It is the beginning of a divine union of two people, as well as a union of two families. It is also a step toward higher goals in life, from taking more responsibility to the opportunity to grow materially and spiritually.

Human life is experienced in three states: physical, composed of matter and energy; subtle, composed of mind, intelligence and ego; and causal, composed of soul and spirit. The beauty of the Vedic ceremonies lies in the fact that they invoke the union of two individuals at all three states of human experience.

Vedic ceremonies are performed in Sanskrit, the most ancient surviving Indo-European language. It is very important to realize that, at the core of a Vedic marriage, lies emphasis on the two essential values of harmony and growth; these are the values most cherished in a Hindu household, and are considered the two pillars of a happy and healthy society.

Harmony, beginning with one's inner self and encompassing the whole of creation, remains at the heart of all the ceremonies performed, since it is believed that true peace for any individual is only possible when harmony prevails around and within.

Samskaras can also be viewed as cultural imprints.And since childhood is the most impressionable age, most samskaras are given during this of one's life.

The householder's life is an opportunity for the couple to grow spiritually together by learning to merge their individual "I - consciousness" (*Ahankara*) and evolve their "We - consciousness" (*Vayamkara*). Vedic rituals and ceremonies evoke divine will for the growth of the couple.

As you perform these ceremonies and rituals, you will realize that they all aim at fulfilling these two core values.

Sixteen Hindu Samskaras

1. Impregnation
2. Fetus protection
3. Satisfying the cravings of pregnant mother
4. Child birth
5. Giving the child name
6. First outing of the child from home
7. Giving the child solid food
8. Shaving the child's head
9. Piercing the child's ear
10. Investing with the sacred thread
11. Starting the study of Vedas
12. Returning home after completing education
13. Marriage
14. Invoking ancestors
15. *Vanprastha and Sanyasa*
16. Cremation

In a "Gandharv Vivah" the couple could get married without the priest by performing the ceremony keeping fire as a witness.

How Long Will it Take?

An Overview of the Ceremony

A Hindu marriage ceremony is based on Vedas, the most ancient scriptures in the world. That is why it is called a "Vedic" ceremony. The ceremony has evolved over thousands of years. It has been said that Lord Ram and Sita were married according to Vedic ceremonies.

However, as you perform the Vedic ceremony, it is important to keep in mind the difference between rituals and customs. Though the rituals described here are thousands of years old and each has a specific significance in the Hindu view of life, customs have evolved in different parts of India, in different castes, and even in different families. We have focused on those rituals that form an integral part of all Hindu weddings, regardless of caste or region. We aim to ensure that you understand and enjoy this rich cultural aspect of Hindu culture fully, and do not get side-tracked by indigenous customs.

Although traditionally the ceremony took several days, today a typical ceremony lasts for only about two hours from the time the *"vara yatra"* (groom's procession) arrives to when the couple leaves for the groom's house. Having said that, some of the rituals start a couple of days before the actual wedding day when Lord Ganesh is invoked in both homes and blessings are sought from Ganesh to make the forthcoming event auspicious and free from obstacles.

Although not of religious significance, the night before the wedding is usually a very important and enjoyable event, celebrated as a music night, when relatives, friends and family members get together, sing wedding songs, play *garba* (a folk dance of Gujarat) or *bhangra* (a folk dance from Punjab) and enjoy themselves.

19

The wedding day itself starts with both bride and groom getting ready in their respective households usually helped by their aunts and other relatives who apply *pithi* (a yellow paste made by mixing turmeric powder and *chandan - a fragrant paste of sandal wood*).

At the groom's house, after the *pithi* has been applied, the groom's procession prepares to go to the wedding venue. This *vara yatra* usually features the groom riding a horse, a live band, and dancing by the groom's friends and family members.

When the *vara yatra* reaches the bride's house or hall, her mother and family receive it. The bride's mother greets the groom with *arati*, *tilak* and the throwing of *akshat* (rice).

Order of Events

Ganesh Poojan:

A few days before the wedding, a special place in the home of both the bride and the groom is established by invoking the Lord Ganesh. Ganesh is believed to remove obstacles so that the wedding can be performed without any bad or unexpected events.

Mandap
photo courtsey Nalini Creations

Mandaparohana:

Establishing a place to perform the wedding ceremony takes place at the bride's house or at the wedding hall.

20

Welcoming the Vara yatra

When the groom and his party arrive at the wedding hall, the bride's parents, family and friends meet them. The groom is usually greeted at the hall with *arati* performed by the mother of the bride, followed by *tilak*, grains of *akshat*, and a garland.

Jaymala (Fresh flower necklace):

At the beginning of the ceremony, the bride and groom exchange fresh flower necklaces.

Grahashanti (Peace with the planets):

A ceremony is performed before the wedding to invoke the nine planets by name, receiving blessings from each one for the new couple's life.

Madhuparka Vidhi:

At the *Vedi* the groom is given honey and milk as a welcome and his feet are washed to show respect.

Bringing the Bride:

Usually, the maternal uncle or brother leads the bride into the *mandap* (canopy under which the ceremony is performed) where the groom

Ganesh Kumbha Pujan

and the bride's parents are waiting.

Often guests who are not familiar with the Vedic ceremony may feel at a loss when the ceremony is going on. Let them know beforehand how long will the ceremony last and their role - if any - in the ceremony.

Kanyadan:

The parents of the bride offer their daughter in marriage to the groom.

Panigrahan (hastamilap):

The groom and the bride's right hands are joined, indicating that the groom is now taking the bride as his wife.

Mangalfera:

The bride and the groom circle the fire four times – the number varies from three to seven in different parts of India – as their hands are joined, signifying that they will now be entering into the world together.

Saptapadi:

The bride and groom take seven vows, which seal the marriage forever. These seven vows in Sanskrit and their meaning in English are detailed later in this chapter under "understanding the significance".

Dhruvadarshan:

Vedi

The newly-weds now look at the pole star, known for its steadfastness in the sky. *Dhruvadarshan* signifies that the couple will remain steady and loyal to each other throughout their lives.

Ashirvadam:

The newly-weds now receive blessings from the priest, parents, and elderly members of both the families.

Bidai:

The groom's party, along with the bride, leave to go to the groom's home.

Vadhupravesh:

The welcoming of the newly-weds at the groom's home by his family and relatives.

Hastamilan

What Does it All Mean?

Understanding the Significance

During the preparation of your wedding you will come across many unfamiliar terms and concepts. For example, you may be told that the ceremony has to be performed at time of it's "muhurt". You may be baffled by the term as well the significance of the *muhurt*.

To properly understand Hindu marriage ceremonies you will have to understand the values Hindus traditionally consider essential for good family life. Marriage reinforces the importance of the extended family – for the Hindus, the whole world is one family – and harmony. A Hindu wedding prescribes ritual functions for all important family relationships. Family members from near and far gather for a wedding to perform their roles, and there are special ceremonies to invoke the spirits of ancestors to bless the new couple.

A ceremony starts at the most auspicious time for the couple, called *muhurt*. *Muhurt* is chosen by reference to the time of year and the horoscopes of the couple. The idea is to begin a new journey when the stars and the entire cosmos provide positive vibrations.

Each ceremony described here has a special significance - be it astrological, ecological, or emotional.

Ganesh poojan (veneration to Lord Ganesh)

For Hindus, any auspicious event like a marriage – and all the *samskaras* in one's life – begins with prayers and offerings to Lord Ganesh.

Ganesh represents cosmic intelligence and wisdom. He is The Lord of all new beginnings, the provider of wisdom. His name is invoked at the start of all undertakings and is inscribed at the beginning of all literary works and invitations. Ganesh is the keeper of the threshold, the remover of obstacles, master of the mind and the son of Lord Shiva and Goddess Parvati.

Muhurt:

The selection of an auspicious day and time, determined based on the most favorable configuration of the cosmos, signifies that each one of us is an integral part of the entire cosmos, and that a universal cosmic law governs us all. Thus, an auspicious time of marriage is believed to enhance harmony in the life of the newly-weds. It is also acknowledging our dependence on the higher forces of nature.

Within the marriage ceremony, different *muhurts* are chosen for different parts of the ceremony. For example, *ganesh pooja*, which usually takes place a day or two before the marriage, is carried out at a time chosen by the priest. The same is true for *seherabandi* (tying of the hairpiece for the wedding) for the groom.

Mandap:

Vedic ceremonies are performed within a *mandap*, a symbol of the universe, where the newly weds receive blessings from the guardians of the world. The *mandap* represents the cosmos, where nine poles represent the planets. The guardians of the eight quarters of the universe are:

Indra, Agni, Yama, Nivrit, Varuna, Vayu, Kubera, Isana.

The center pole signifies marriage or *skambha*.

Traditionally, the groom sits on the right hand of the two seats placed on the west side of the fire (*havan kund*). The bride's priest sits on the south side facing north, and groom's priest sits on the east side facing west. The bride's parents sit on the south side facing north. The father of the bride sits closest to her. Her maternal uncle escorts the bride to the *mandap*.

Agni

Vedic ceremonies are performed near a small fire which serves as a witness to the proceedings. *Agni* (fire) symbolizes purity and sacrifice in life.

Agni is believed to have a threefold composition, divine, human and earthly. *Agni* is *adhidaivik*, which represents the non-physical world; *adhyatmic*, which represents the spiritual world; and *adhibhautic*, which represents the material world. It signifies purification and enlightenment. *Agni* is also considered a vehicle for offering because it consumes what is offered.

Vara Yatra (Barat):

Traditionally, the procession of the groom's relatives, friends, and family members goes to the bride's house amidst music, singing, dancing and celebration. In America, the *barat* usually starts at the entrance of the hall and is greeted by the bride's mother and her family. It has become customary for the groom to ride a decorated horse, a tradition from the days when a horse was the chosen means of transportation.

Panigrahan (hastamilap):

Panigrahan literally means "accepting the hands". When the groom takes the bride's right hand in his right hand, he takes her as his wife and undertakes responsibility for her future well-being.

Mangalfera (Laja Homa):

Circling the *Agni* four times by the couple is considered an auspicious beginning for them to start their new life together. According to some experts, each circle signifies one aspect of the Hindu *ashram*.

Kanyadan:

In *Vedic* law, *kanyadan* (giving away of the bride) is considered the highest form of pious duty performed by the parents of the bride. The concept behind *kanyadan* is that the bride is a form of the Goddess Laxmi and the groom is Lord Narayan himself. The parents facilitate the union of these two.

During *kanyadan*, the groom holds his hands open, and the bride lays her half-open hands in his. Over their hands, the father of the bride holds his open palm at an angle, while the mother of the bride pours water on her husband's hand which falls on the hands of bride and the groom. The rituals of *kanyadan* and *panigrahan* are combined while the priest chants *mantras*.

Jay Mala

Manglashtak:

The priest and both families recite eight verses, written in traditional form especially for the couple. The verses are often composed by family members and invoke Lord Ganesh, *Ishtadevata* (personal deity), *Kuldevata* (family deity) and ancestors, so all of them may come and bless the couple. We have provided a sample *manglashtak* in Sanskrit and Gujarati for you to use if you wish. You may want to customize the verses to fit your specific wedding.

Saptapadi:

Saptapadi (the seven vows taken by bride and groom) is one of the most ancient ceremonies. It is a crucial part of the ceremony that validates a marriage. The vows are taken by the couple around the ceremonial fire. Here are the actual *mantras* in Sanskrit and their meaning.

ॐ इषे एक पदी भव सामां अनुव्रता भव ।

विष्णुः स्वा नयतु पुत्रान् विदावहै बहूंस्ते सन्तु जरद् अष्टयः ।

ॐ ऊर्जें द्विपदी भव ।

ॐ रायस्पोषाय त्रिपदी भव ।

ॐ मयोभवाय चतुष्पदी भव ।

ॐ प्रजाभ्यः पंचपदी भव ।

ॐ ऋतुभ्यः षटपदी भव ।

ॐ सखे सप्तपदी भव ।

Groom:

1. My beloved, our love became firm by your walking one step with me. You will offer me the food and be helpful in every way. I will cherish you and provide for the welfare and happiness of you and our children.

2. My beloved, now you have walked the second step with me, fill my heart with strength and courage and together we shall protect the household and children.

3. My beloved, now you have walked three steps with me. By virtue of this, our wealth and prosperity is going to grow. I shall look upon all other women as my sisters. Together, we will educate our children and may they live long.

4. My beloved, it is a great blessing that you have walked four steps with me. You have brought auspiciousness and sacredness into my life. May we be blessed with obedient and noble children. May they live long.

5. My beloved, now you have walked five steps with me. You have enriched my life. May God bless you. May our loved ones live long and share in our prosperity.

6. My beloved, you have filled my heart with happiness by walking six steps with me. May you be filled with peace for all time.

7. My beloved, as you walked the seven steps with me, our love and friendship became eternal. We experienced spiritual union in God. Now you have become completely mine and I offer my life to you. Our marriage will be forever.

Bride:

1. My lord, I will love you with single minded devotion as my husband. I will treat all other men as my brothers. My devotion to you is of a chaste wife and you are my joy. This is my commitment and my pledge to you.

Mangal fera

2. My lord, in your grief, I shall fill your heart with courage and strength. In your happiness, I shall rejoice, I promise you that I will please you always with sweet words and take care of the family and children. And you shall love me and me alone as your wife.

Antarpat, a piece of cloth used between the bride and the groom during the initial part of the ceremony is evident in many parts of India and it may suggest that bride and groom have not seen each other yet.

3. My lord, I will love you with single minded devotion as my husband, I will treat all other men as my brothers. My devotion to you is of a chaste wife and you are my joy. This is my commitment and my pledge to you.

4. My lord, I will decorate you from feet to your head with flowers, garlands and ornaments and anoint you with sandalwood paste and fragrance. I will serve you and please you in every way I can.

5. My lord, I share both in your joys and sorrows. Your love will make me trust and honor you. I will carry our your wishes.

6. My lord, in all acts of righteousness, in every form of enjoyment and divine acts, I promise you I shall participate and I shall always be with you.

7. My lord, as God and the Holy Scriptures, I have become your spouse. Whatever promises we gave, we have spoken in pure mind. We will be truthful to each other in all things. We will love each other forever.

Understanding *Saptapadi* in Today's Context

It may be difficult for today's young people to take vows that do not seem consistent with their lifestyles, and appreciate the context in which *saptapadi* was created thousands of years ago. The beauty of these vows is that they are as relevant today as in ancient times. The only requirement is to understand the vows you will take in the context of the kind of life you will live.

Here we offer the same *saptapadi* with the same meaning as the *mantras* but more consistent with today's lifestyle.

Step One (Sharing):

We promise to share the duties and welfare of the family. We will respect each other. We will take care of each other's well being, both material and spiritual.

Step Two (Family *Dharma*):

We will share each other's joys and sorrows with courage and strength. Together, we will protect and provide for our family.

Step Three (Harmonious Life):

We take an oath of trust and loyalty to each other. We believe this will ensure prosperity, joy of life, and longevity. Our great standards of morality will allow us to raise children with noble character.

Step Four (Growth):

We will develop a love for beauty, art, literature and will fill each other's life with fragrance for human values: love, compassion, understanding, sacrifice, and service.

Step Five (Restatement):

Let us reconfirm our four vows of purity, love, family duties, harmony and growth.

Step Six (Spiritual Development and social obligations):

We will conduct our lives according to the principles of *dharma*. We will perform all acts of righteousness. We will continue the great traditions of our *dharma* and pass on these eternal values to our children. We will ensure the continuation of our great Hindu heritage for the benefit of all humanity.

Step Seven (Eternal Bond):

Now with these seven steps, we are related as husband and wife and our bond is eternal. Let our love and friendship become eternal.

31

We have accepted each other in the presence of God, our ancestors, our parents, our relatives and friends. We will abide by our *Vedic* scriptures.

Finally, both bride and groom take a vow:
"Having taken these seven steps together, I assure you that I will not swerve from the path of my love and friendship with you. So should you also not swerve. Let our thoughts, decisions and actions be one and in unison. Let us be kind, loving, considerate, good and open hearted to each other. Let us share food, possessions, strength and advantages together. Let us be complementary to each other as thought and speech are to each other."

Sindur Dan or Mang Bharai:

The *sindur dan* ceremony involves the application of vermilion powder with *akshat*, to the mid-hair parting of the bride. It is performed by the groom.
Soon after the groom has applied the powder, the priests bless them by throwing *akshat* and chanting *mantras* from the Vedas. This is to signify the change of status from bride to wife.

Dhruva Darshan:

Hindu marriages signify a mystical union of man's creative ambitions and woman's supportive strengths. At the end of these ceremonies, the priest guides the couple to look at the pole star. Historically, the pole star has guided people at night since it stays fixed in the sky.

Purnahuti:

The bride is auspicious, a harbinger of all good. See her one and all; admire and bless her with your best wishes that she be happy and prosperous in life. Bless her before you disperse.

In a Hindu concept of marriage, the bride and groom take the vows to be complemetary to each other as thought and speech are to each other.

32

Why is it a little different in every family?

Unity in Diversity

Although the core aspects of a Vedic marriage have remained essentially the same for thousands of years, *Vedic* ceremonies have evolved differently in various parts of India and also in each sect, sub-sect or even in each family. The Sikh and Jain religions, for example, are off-shoots of Hindu religion so their core ceremony is based on *Vedic* ceremony, however, there are differences in the way the ceremony is performed. Similarly, each region has it's own unique celebration. These customs and rituals create a richness and variety that is the most essential and integral aspect of Hindu way of life. Some customs have evolved because of the environment. For example, Indians living in America may develop a custom of exchanging rings reflecting the influence of the host culture.

In this chapter, we have tried to capture the uniqueness of various parts of India. Please note that this is by no means a comprehensive description of all the differences, but rather an attempt to show how they all have retained the core values of *Vedic* ceremony while highlighting inherent uniqueness.

Sikh Couple

Sikh Wedding:

The Sikh wedding ceremony is called *Anand Karaj*, a "ceremony of bliss", and is performed according to the Anand Act of 1909. The ceremony is usually conducted at a Sikh *gurudwara* or at the bride's home and is officiated by a respected member of the Sikh community. Sikh weddings exhibit an exuberant, enthusiastic approach to life which is a trademark of Punjab, the state where Sikhism originated.

A traditional Sikh wedding begins with the groom riding a horse from his house to the bride's, taking with him his friends and relatives in a procession. The bride usually wears a pink salwar-kameez with gold designs and the groom wears a bright red or pink turban.

Activities usually start weeks before the wedding and the wedding home is filled with happy vibrations. The formal ceremonies begin with *sagan*, in which the families exchange gifts and confirm the engagement. Singing and dancing take place every night until the wedding. Before the actual ceremony begins, the bride's parents welcome the groom and his parents with flowers.

The wedding ceremony consists of four holy verses from the *Granth Sahib*. They explain the obligations of married life, and while the verses are sung, the groom takes the bride in a ceremonial walk around the Holy Book for four *lavans*.

These ceremonies are particular to a Sikh wedding:

Churha (bangle ceremony): the bride's maternal aunt and uncle cover the bride's wrist with white and red bangles. Light ornaments of beaten silver and gold called *kalira* are tied to the bangles. The bride and the groom sit in front of the *Granth Sahib*, the holy book of the Sikhs. The ceremony of the circumambulation of the *Granth Sahib* ends with the reading of the *ardas*, a rousing salutation to the ten Gurus of the Sikhs.

Doli: At the end of the ceremony, there is a farewell to the bride as she leaves her parent's home. The bride throws a handful of *akshat* over her shoulder, signifying that prosperity will still continue even after the *laxmi* of the house is gone.

Jain Wedding:

Jainism has its roots in Hinduism and Jain weddings are essentially similar to Hindu weddings with a few special differences. Here are the steps to a Jain wedding ceremony.

Jain Marriage Rites

Vagdana - The parents of both bride and groom declare their children's intention to marry. This is, essentially, an engagement ceremony.

Pradana - The groom's parents offer ornaments and other items as gifts to the future bride.

Mandap-vedi-pratishtha - Making the *mandap* and the *vedi* for the ceremony is an important aspect of the wedding ceremony and is done at a special time.

Toran-pratishtha - installing the ornament.

Vara-yatra - the groom rides the horse to the bride's home.

Toran-vidhi - Rites at the gate.

Gotrocchhara - Reciting the *gotras*, or genealogies

Paraspara-mukha-avalokana - Looking at each other's face

Varamala - a thread garland.

Vara-pratiJina - the vows

Agni-pradakshina - circling the sacred fire

Kanyadan - Father gives away his daughter

Devashastra-Guru puja - Worship of Jina, Gurus, and the Scriptures

Vaskshepa - Fragrant material placed in the fire

Granthi-bandhana - Tying the knot

Pani-grahana - The groom takes the bride's hand as a symbol of taking her in his care.

Saptapadi - The seven steps, each one with a vow, often called *agni-pradakshina*.

Ashirvada - Giving blessings.

Sva-graha-agamana - Coming to the groom's house

Jina-grahe-danarpana - Donating to the temple and other institutions.

Punjabi Wedding:

In Punjab, weddings are a very colorful and joyous events where the entire extended family and the neighborhood participate. Weddings are filled with music, dancing, and eating for many days.

A particular specialty of a Punjabi wedding is *milni*, in which, soon after the *barat* arrives, each side of the family greets the other side with fresh garlands of flowers. The brother of the bride greets the brother of the groom, the father of the bride greets the father of the groom, the grandfather of the bride greets the grandfather of the groom and so on. The custom of *milni* is unique to Punjabi weddings and reinforces the Hindu value of emphasis on family life.

The *kangana ki rasam* (amulet tying ceremony) is very symbolic and a special ceremony is performed. An amulet is made of hand-spun and dyed yarn and several items, such as an iron ring, a *supari (beetlenut)*, mustard seeds wrapped in red piece of cloth and a sea shell, are tied to it. This is done the day before the wedding.

Bride

Marathi Wedding:

In a Marathi wedding, an essential aspect is *manglashtak* which is written and sung to invoke *kuldevata* and other gods to bless the bride and groom.

When the *vara yatra (barat)* arrives at the bride's house or the wedding hall, the groom is welcomed by the bride's mother who performs *arati* and *tilak* on his forehead. Soon afterwards, when the groom is seated in the *mandap*, the bride's maternal uncle brings her there. At the start of the ceremony, the bride sits on the right hand side of the groom. After *saptapadi*, the bride moves to the left side, signifying that now she resides in the heart of her husband.

One of the most significant parts of a Marathi wedding is the offering of *mangalsutra* (a black beaded necklace with a special gold pendant) to the bride by the groom. Most married women from Maharashtra wear *mangalsutra* all the time, and consider it very auspicious.

Marathi Couple

Gujarati Wedding:

Gujarati weddings highlight some playful customs of their own. Upon the arrival of the *vara yatra (barat)*, bride's mother greets the groom; she performs *arati* and tries to grab his nose. This is a playful reminder that he has finally come rubbing his nose at their door asking for their daughter in marriage.

Madhuparka is an integral part of Gujarati wedding, where the groom's feet are washed and he is fed honey and milk while sitting under the *mandap*.

One often carried out playful event in a Gujarati wedding is the stealing of the groom's shoes by the bride's sister. At the end of the ceremony, the groom has to offer a token gift to recover them.

Varamala is performed before the *kanyadan*. In *varamala*, the elders of the house place a cord around the couple's necks to protect them from evil influences.

The *mangalfera* (going around the fire) is followed by a ceremony called *saubhagyavati bhava*. In this ceremony, seven married women from the bride's family whisper blessings into the right ear of the bride.

Upon arrival at the groom's house, the couple is greeted by the groom's sisters who refuses to let the brother enter the house. This ceremony is called *barnu rokvu,* and is performed in many other regions of India as well.

Gujarati Bride

Tamil Wedding:

Wedding ceremonies in the south of India seem to have remained closer to their Hindu origins.

A typical Tamil wedding starts with *kashiyatra* where the groom is persuaded to become a householder by the bride's father convincing him that he should get married instead of making a pilgimage to *Kashi* (the holy city of Bhagvan Shri Vishwanath) Although there is no *vara yatra (barat)* by that name, something similar takes place when the groom goes to the temple or wedding hall.

On the morning of the wedding, both bride and groom are given an oil bath. Then the groom goes through *samskar* ceremonies to ensure that he has received all the *samskaras* before the wedding. Then both bride and groom sit on a swing where they exchange garlands. Next, the groom's mother takes the bride to the *mandap* and the bride's mother takes the groom to the *mandap* for the ceremony.

The actual ceremony consists of groom's *pooja* (for a Hindu, the groom represents Lord Vishnu), *kanyadan, panigrahan,* and *saptapadi.* After the *saptapadi,* there is a ceremony called *mangalya dharma,* where the bride is given *mangalsutra* as a token of being a married woman. Typically the cost of the *mangalsutra* is borne equally by both families. A toe-ring ceremony is performed by the bride's maternal aunt, who puts a ring on the bride's second toe. When night falls, the couple is shown the pole and *arundhati* stars as symbols of stability and faithfulness.

Kashmiri Wedding:

In the northern state of Kashmir, the wedding ceremony begins a few days before the wedding with house cleaning (*livun*). On this and subsequent days up to *mehandirat* (the application of henna designs to the bride's hands and feet), neighborhood women and girls come to the bride's house for *sangeet* (music). The most common instrument used is a long-necked clay drum, open on one end, called a *tumbak nari*. Its unique sound announces that a special ceremony is being held.

Mehandirat is a night long ceremony of music, dance, food and drink.

Devagoon On the morning following *mehandirat*, this ceremony is performed to seek blessings for the preparation and purification of the future bride and groom.

On the wedding day, the bride's parents receive the *barat*. Before entering the *mandap,* the bride and the groom stand on a *yoog*, a circle made on the ground decorated with various designs and colors. The mother of the bride brings a *thali* (a large plate) with sweets and flowers (symbolizing happiness and prosperity), and puts a piece of *burfee* (a sweet made from cheese) in the groom's mouth. The groom bites on it and the same piece is then put in the mouth of the bride and she does the same. This is done three times.

The bride and the groom are then led to the *mandap* where the priest performs the ceremony, with *saptapadi* being the centerpiece.

One of the unique customs of a Kashmiri wedding is *pooshi puza* or flower worship. Two people hold a long piece of cloth over the heads of the bride and groom and the relatives of the bride present shower flower petals on the cloth, accompanied by *Vedic* chanting by the priest. This is done for fifteen to twenty minutes and by the time it is over, the bride and the groom find themselves covered with a layer of flowers several inches thick. The showering of flowers symbolizes the giving up of the daughter by her parents to the custody of her husband. The ceremony is magnificent.

When the bride and the groom leave the *mandap* after final blessings, the groom finds that a group of small children from the bride's side have stolen his shoes.

The bride and the groom now go to groom's house where the bride is dressed by the groom's parents in new clothes and jewelry.

40

Bengali Wedding:

In a Bengali wedding, the bride's family asks permission of the groom's family to begin the ceremony. Pretending to see each other for the first time, the bride circles the groom while his face is covered with a fine piece of cloth. Then they both exchange fresh flower garlands.

Now the ceremony starts. The fire is lit in the *vedi* and *saptapadi* is performed. One of the most significant rituals in a Bengali wedding is the *sindur dan*, when the groom puts the *sindur* in the parting of the bride's hair announcing that they are now husband and wife. Traditionally, after the *kanyadan*, the groom's priest takes over, as the couple belongs to the new family.

In America, only one priest usually performs the entire ceremony. After the wedding the newly-weds spend their first night at the bride's house and leave for the groom's house the next morning. At the groom's house, there is a special celebration, where the bride offers *akshat* to everyone in the family and thereby establishes herself as the *bahu* (daughter-in-law) of the family.

Bengali Ceremony

Conclusion:

There are still many other varieties within a Hindu marriage such as Rajasthani and Asamese, that we are unable to include here. However, suffice to say that each one of these ceremonies bring the beauty of its own while keeping the core values intact. You can see how wedding ceremonies of Hindus truly reflect Unity in Diversity.

Sikh Bride

Planning
Guide

First Things First

How to keep your sanity during the planning: Expect that some things will be done differently from how you would wish. Decide what matters the most to you and do not fuss over the rest.

Planning

Planning your wedding is a task that may turn out to be one of the most stressful times of your life. It requires creativity, flexibility, patience and tact. Proper planning is the key. Indeed, the process of planning can be one of concrete anticipation and a time that you will cherish for the rest of your life. Good planning can also ensure that your wedding day is a most memorable day for you and your guests. This chapter will help you make this daunting process manageable and even enjoyable.

First, discuss with your partner and decide on the kind of wedding you would like to have - formal, informal, or something in between. Feel free to think of a wedding which reflects your special interests or hobbies. Once you two have sorted out your thoughts, the first thing you want to do is to inform both the families of your decision. If you think it is necessary, arrange a formal meeting with both the families. You want to begin your new life with the blessings and good wishes of your immediate family members.

Announcement

You set the tone of the entire wedding by how you choose to announce your wedding. Start with a style that suits you. It can range from informal to elaborate. But first make sure that both families have been informed properly. Talk to both sets of parents at homes. Think about the kind of information you would like to share with your family. Choose a quiet time when you will not be disturbed. If you feel comfortable, tell them why you wish to marry – but be tactful. Realize that right now you are charged with emotions.

47

Select two to three possible dates for the wedding. This will give you some flexibility in selecting a hall or finding a priest.

What you need to know about your engagement party:

An engagement party is usually hosted by the bride's family, but can be hosted by both.

It is a perfect opportunity to introduce the families to each other.

Gifts are generally not given, but if they are, accept them graciously and send thank-you notes.

Avoid hurt feelings by inviting only those guests who will also be invited to the wedding.

Planning for the Big Day

Although both of you will be working together to plan for the wedding, each one of you will need to understand and plan things slightly differently since your needs will differ. Here is a separate planning guide for both of you.

Bride:

You have the rest of your life to be married, so take your time and enjoy the pre-wedding parties, shopping and planning before the special day. With proper planning, you can make your wedding day romantic, exciting and memorable not only for you but also for your guests. Keep in mind that the less time you allow yourself, the more flexible you will have to be on dates and timing. Before you decide the date, make sure you allow yourself enough preparation time.

Decide the kind of wedding you would like to have: formal, informal, or somewhere in between.

As soon as dates are settled, tell family and close friends so that date conflicts can be avoided.

Consult a priest if you want a proper *muhurt*.

Reserve the wedding venue six months to a year in advance for a large, formal wedding and three months for a smaller one.

Six to Twelve months before the big day:

Select a wedding date and time.

Establish a preliminary budget.

Select a wedding theme and style that fits your budget.

Select locations for both the ceremony and the reception.

Decide who will officiate at the ceremony. Talk to a few priests and find one who shares your style and philosophy.

Decide on a color scheme.

Decide on the number of guests.

Start compiling the names and addresses of guests.

Select names of the members of the wedding party – family, cousins, best friends.

Bride

Plan the reception.

Decide on a menu and contact caterers.

Select a caterer that meets your style and budget.

Select a professional photographer and a videographer.

If you are getting anything from India, allow much longer time than suggested by the vendor of the shipping company.

Select a florist. Remember that Hindu weddings require lots of flowers! Make a list of your needs; consider your color scheme, the seasonal availability of flowers.

Select a wedding dress.

Select dresses for the members of the wedding party.

Select or buy appropriate jewelry.

Four months before the big day:

Make final arrangement for the ceremony, talk to the priest, pay deposits and sign contracts

Have close relatives select their dresses and jewelry.

Pick a bridal registry close to both families and friends.

Order invitations and stationery.

Finalize the guest list.

Check the state requirements for blood tests and a marriage license.

Make an appointment for a physical examination.

Start planning the honeymoon.

Decide where you will live after the wedding.

Begin shopping for a new house or apartment.

Two months before the big day:

Address the wedding invitations. They should be mailed six to eight weeks before the wedding.

Finalize details with the caterer, photographer, videographer, florist, reception hall manager, musicians and others.

Order the wedding cake.

Make appointments with your hairdresser and beautician.

Arrange accommodations for out-of-town guests and the groom's family and friends.

Finalize plans for the honeymoon.

One month before the big day:

Complete all physical dental appointments.

Get the marriage license and the results of the blood test. (See the section on the marriage license and blood tests.)

Make transportation arrangement for the day.

Purchase the "wedding favor" gifts for the guests.

If the families are to exchange gifts, buy those gifts.

Prepare outfits for going away, and gifts from the family to the bride.

Keep a careful record of all gifts received and write thank-you notes immediately.

Select a responsible person to handle the guest book and decide on its location.

Keep things in perspective - do not make the wedding larger than life so that nobody can enjoy it.

Two weeks before the wedding;

Attend to business and legal details such as change of name, address on social security, driver's license, medical plans, bank accounts and so forth.

Re-confirm accommodations for out-of-town guests and the groom's party.

Start working on seating arrangements.

Contact those guests who have not yet responded.

Reconfirm arrangements with the caterer, hall manager, florist and others.

One week before the wedding:

Mehndi

Give the final guest count to the caterer and review the details.

Give a list of pictures to be taken to the photographer and videographer, familiarize them with important family members and their roles in the wedding.

Give the musicians a list of the music you want played during the reception.

Finalize the seating arrangements – but keep some room for last minute changes.

52

Arrange for someone to help with last minute errands.

Contact your hairdresser and make-up person to determine how much time they will need and plan accordingly. Start packing for the honeymoon.

Make sure you have a marriage license!

Carry out a rehearsal with everyone involved and review their roles.

Stay with your family the night before the wedding. Go to bed early – you will want to look and feel wonderful the next day.

On the Wedding Day:

Relax! You have a big day ahead of you.

Have your hair done at least three to four hours before the ceremony.

Allow enough time for make-up.

Get dressed one and half hours before the wedding so that pictures can be taken.

Have the music start a half-hour before the ceremony to set the tone.

Seat guests in the hall.

Seat relatives in the hall.

Bridal Bouquet

Make sure all of your vendors are given accurate and clear directions to the hall.

Groom:

Six to Twelve months before the wedding day:

Select a wedding date and time.

Start planning and making arrangements for the honeymoon.

Start compiling the names and addresses of guests.

Discuss and plan your living arrangements after wedding with your fiancée.

Select friends for the wedding party.

Four months before the wedding day:

Make final arrangements for the ceremony.

Have close relatives select their clothes and jewelry.

Complete the guest list.

Check state requirements for blood tests and a marriage license.

Groom's Friends in a barat

Make an appointment for a physical examination.

Finalize plans for the honeymoon and pay deposits if required.

Decide where you will live after the wedding.

Select your wedding outfit and those for other occasions.

Three months before the wedding, find a hairdresser and try out your wedding hairstyle. If it doesn't work, your hair will have a chance to grow back.

Two months before the wedding day:

Help your parents when they need it.

Decide how you will arrive at the ceremony. Arrange for a horse and decorations if required. If travelling by car, finalize the details.

Select the music to be played during the procession.

Make rehearsal arrangements.

Arrange accommodations for out-of-town guests.

One month before the wedding day:

Complete all physical and dental appointments.

Get the results of the blood test and obtain a marriage license.

Arrange transportation for the wedding day.

If gifts are to be exchanged by the families, purchase those gifts.

Select clothing for the best men.

Keep a careful record of all the gifts received and write thank-you notes.

Select a responsible person to handle the guests and the guest

Focus on your favorite part of the day. Is it the ceremony, reception, seeing your friends? Whatever it is, focus on that rather than what could go wrong.

book, and arrange the location of the guest book.

Two weeks before the wedding day:

Attend to business and legal matters such as adding the bride's name to insurance policies, medical plans, bank accounts and other legal documents.

Re-confirm the arrangements for out-of-town guests.

Contact guests who have not yet responded.

One week before the wedding day:

Give the final guest count to the caterer and review details.

Go over final details with all professional services and inform them of any changes.

Give the photographer and videographer the list of pictures you want.

Give the musicians the music list for reception.

Finalize the seating arrangements.

Arrange with someone to help with last minute errands.

Pack for the honeymoon.

Contact your hairdresser and determine how much time he or she needs.

If you have guests coming from India or any other country, request them to come at least a week or two prior to the wedding day. That gives them a chance to get over the jetlag and get used to the weather.

If you are flying, make sure you have your plane tickets, visa, passport and other documentation.

Arrange for gifts to be taken to your home after the reception.

Stay with your family the night before the wedding. Go to bed early – you will want to look and feel your very best the next day.

Sacred Coconut

On the Day:

Allow plenty of time to dress.

Arrive on time.

Arrange for the wedding certificate to be signed by a witness.

Thank the bride's parents before leaving the reception hall and say good-bye to everyone.

Take good care of your new bride.

Designing Your Wedding

Details...Details...Details

As it is said, the difference between extra ordinary and ordinary is that little extra. By taking care of all the seemingly small details, by going that extra mile, you can enhance the quality of your wedding day -for yourself as well as for your guests - by many folds. This chapter will help you think through the process in detail to add, delete, or customize various things in your wedding. Use this chapter for planning for every detail but also feel free to add your special touch while planning.

Announcement

In a Hindu wedding, families of both bride and groom play a very active and vital role, and it is probably they who decide how

Ice sculpture of Ganesh

to make the announcement. However, you may choose to have a small party for your friends to announce your decision. Before you make a formal announcement, discuss basic details with your parents, such as if and when you are planning to have an engagement party, and a tentative wedding date. You do not have to be specific at this stage.

Your parents may decide to have a party to announce the happy news. This can be as simple as an informal gathering of close friends and relatives. For many Hindu families, this is the time to exchange coconuts and small token gifts. Such gifts are often silver coins with vermilion. They are exchanged in a ceremony that includes putting *tilak* on the couple as an acknowledgment of welcoming them into their families.

Alternatively, you may decide to have a more traditional announcement with a small party or may chose to simply inform close relatives and friends by phone or email. The choice is yours.

A word about engagement parties.

If you live close to each other, one engagement party will probably fulfill your needs. During the party you may have a small *vidhi* (ceremony) with a priest where both of you do some *pooja* of your family deity in front of your guests and exchange small gifts.

You can use your engagement party as a test run for your caterer and other wedding suppliers.

Here are some of the things to consider in your engagement party.

Are you going to have a ceremony? If yes, have you talked to the priest? (Try to keep the ceremony short and symbolic.)

Are you or the families planning to exchange gifts? If so, how and when?

Are you planning speeches? If you are, who will deliver them and for how long?

How will you introduce the families to each other?

Gift Registries

Should you start a bridal registry at local stores?

The answer may differ according to your belief system, the size and style of your wedding and other factors. You will both have to decide how you feel about having one. There are advantages

When engaging a photographer, double check the time allowed, or you may end up paying overtime if the ceremony or reception runs longer than anticipated.

Add a nice authentic touch by selecting at least one traditional wedding dish in your dinner menu. For example, in Gujarat, "kansar" - a sweet - is traditionally served to the couple during the ceremony. You can add that to your menu along with another sweet.

and disadvantages to registering.

The most obvious advantage is being able to select what you will receive, thus eliminating a lot of guess work for your guests. You can be confident that your gifts will not be duplicated or unwanted.

On the other hand, many people feel uncomfortable telling their guests what to buy, where to buy it and how much to spend (within limits). There is another reason. You may spend much time selecting what you would like, only to discover that many of your guests have already chosen gifts themselves.

If you decide to have gift registration, there are several things to consider:

Select more than one store so that your different needs are addressed.

If many of your guests are from out of town, make sure you select one or two stores local to them.

*R*egister for items across a range of prices so guests can purchase gifts within their budgets.

Choose a theme for your registry. If you both have a passion for something, for example, music, pick a music store for your registry. Book stores, antique shops, garden shops – they will all be more than happy to have you register.

Location

Your choice of venue will speak volumes about you and your wedding. It is one of the most crucial decisions you will have to make early on in the planning. Besides availability and cost, your choice will be based on a number of factors.

How far are you willing to travel?

Ideally, you will want to select a place that is not too far from your home. Traveling more than half an hour on your wedding day may create problems.

How many guests are you planning to invite?

This will be the most important factor in selecting a venue. Talk to both families and decide on an agreeable number. Most Indian weddings have a larger number of guests than traditional Western weddings, so many venues may not be suitable.

What kind of atmosphere do you want?

Your wedding will take on an aura from the venue. For example, it would be difficult to have an informal wedding in a formal country club. The atmosphere of the location will become an integral part of your wedding ceremony.

Does the facility have a fire certificate?

Since a Hindu wedding incorporates a small fire, make sure that the hall you choose is aware of this.

Can you use outside caterers?

Indian weddings often have special dietary requirements, so make certain that the hall allows you to have an outside caterer.

Does the facility allow children?

You will doubtless have children on your guest list, so find out what facilities the proposed venue provides for children.

There are other considerations you will need to discuss, such as what is included in the charge and what is not, if there any other events happening at the time of your wedding, maintenance, staffing and so on.

If you are offering food at a station at the reception and your guests are lining up, check out the floor layout so there is no confusion.

Selecting a priest

If you live in a large metropolitan area, you will probably have a wide choice of priests. If so, meet with several and, if possible, watch them perform a ceremony.

It is important that your priest understands, and can explain, the significance of important rituals. He will be largely responsible for the kind of environment that is created around the canopy - from the authenticity of the ceremony to the mood of the bride and groom. Talk with your priest at length.

Find out:

If he is performing more than one ceremony that day. If so, this may delay his arrival or he may rush your wedding to attend another.

If he can officiate at ceremonies before and after the wedding, such as the ceremony at the groom's house before he leaves for the wedding, or after the newly-weds arrive at the house.

If he is going to perform the ceremony in English (the actual *slokas* are in Sanskrit), then check his English pronunciation. This is particularly important in interracial marriages or if the majority of your guests do not understand the Indian language the priest might use.

If his overall style suits yours. For example, if you are planning a very formal wedding, you will want a priest whose style is formal.

Catering Services

The second most important item to choose, after the wedding hall, is the kind of food you will serve at your wedding. By selecting the right kind of caterer you will create the atmosphere you

Consider who should be signing the invitation cards beforehand since in a Hindu tradition grandparents and other family members names are often included in the invitiation.

62

want. It is also one of most expensive items on your list, so choose wisely.

Fortunately, of all the wedding services that are available today for an Indian wedding in America, catering probably offers the most choice. You can choose from small, home-based operations to large restaurants, and everything in between.

Certain traditional dishes are associated with Hindu weddings. If you can find a caterer that offers such items, you will be able to add a special touch to your wedding.

Guest Book

Though it is entirely optional, we highly recommend having one, as it will create a delightful memory of this happy day. You can find suitable guest books in stationary stores, jewelry stores and bridal shops. Assign a person who can gently remind guests to sign their names.

Bridal shower:

Although bridal showers are not an Indian tradition, most wedding in America are preceded by a bridal shower. Bridal showers are given by bride's friends or mother and other female relatives and since you do not have to be planning for it, we are not discussing it in much more detail here.

Invitations

For most of your guests, the invitation is the first they will know of your marriage, so ensure that the invitations match the style of your wedding. For example, if you are planning a very formal wedding, an invitation with casual language and style is clearly inappropriate.

Consider the language you use very carefully, or have a professional writer help you. Have family members or friends proofread the invitation so no grammatical or typographical errors are in-

Order a few extra invitations. It will be cheaper than having them special ordered afterwards.

If possible, offer a sit-down dinner with waiters serving the food instead of a buffet dinner. This makes your guests feel like guests and reinforces the Hindu idea of "treating your guests like God".

cluded.

Although parents and even grandparents traditionally sign invitations, it is up to you to decide who to invite. You may wish to have two different invitation cards, one for your friends and one for family friends and relatives.

Who to Invite?

Who to invite is a complicated decision and should be handled with tact. Keep in mind that, in a Hindu wedding, parents play a vital role and the guest list will include many of their friends whom you may not know. For parents, it is "their" celebration for their child's wedding. Relax and enjoy. Do not make an issue of this.

Photography and Videography

Your wedding will be remembered by you, others involved, and even future generations, by the pictures and the video taken at the wedding. So choose your photographer and your videographer with care. Look at their previous work and make sure that their styles match yours. For example, if you are planning a large, elegant wedding and your photographer specializes in small, intimate wedding, he may not be the best match for you.

Make sure your photographer and your videographer know what to expect. Supply written copies of all the ceremonies, timing and the kind of group pictures you want.

Identify family members and close friends with whom you want pictures taken. Select a time between the ceremony and the reception, and advise friends and family members to be available at that time for pictures.

For pictures of the two of you, select interior and exterior locations in advance. Plan for good as well as bad weather. Have these pictures taken a few hours before the wedding, soon after you are ready.

During the reception, make certain to visit every table with a photographer so that you have a picture of each guest sitting at the table with you both.

For your guests, consider placing a disposable camera on each table for them to take impromptu pictures. This may be a good way to get pictures from your guests' points of view. Remember to assign someone to collect the exposed films after the reception.

Wedding Dress:

Of course, you want to look your best in your wedding and your outfit will be a very important and time consuming selection for you. Typical wedding dress for the bride differs from state to state in India and often changes according to fashion. Luckily, in an Indian wedding there are many different kinds of dresses to choose from. So try out various styles and colors before selecting your outfit.

Start by finding out what is traditional in your family, and what different styles are available. If possible, travel to India to see the latest fashions.

Most importantly, select something that suits you and your style of wedding. Just because a traditional bride wears lots of gold threads in her sari does not necessarily mean that you have to follow suit. If you would prefer a simple but elegant outfit, feel free to consider one. Use your judgment and taste and keep in mind that this is a special event for you.

Groom's Wedding Outfit:

In different parts of India, different costumes are popular, but

To the Groom: Avoid wearing western clothes. They make you look out of place and are less functional for some of the rituals you will be performing.

Select an invitation card that properly communicates the style of your wedding.

If possible , consider having a calligrapher write your invitation cards and thank-you notes. It will add style to your wedding.

there are some norms that most people follow. In the north, grooms wear a *sherwani* with a *Churidar* pajama, a *bandha gala* suit or a western style suit. Grooms also wear *sehera*, a veil of flowers tied to the turban to ward off the evil eye.

Keep in mind the kinds of body movement you may need to perform during the ceremony. For example, if you are planning to ride a horse during the *vara yatra (barat)*, your outfit should allow you to lift your leg comfortably while mounting on the horse.

Bride's Wedding Outfit:

The style of bridal outfit depends on the part of India the bride comes from. Most brides wear a sari. In Gujarat, the bride wears a white sari with red design on it, called *panetar* While in Punjab and many northern states the bride wears a red sari with a gold design. A Rajasthani bride would wear a *lehenga*, a Punjabi bride a *salwar-kameez* and a Marathi bride a nine-yard sari.

Flower Girls and Ring bearers:

Although not part of a traditional Hindu wedding, the addition of a flower girl spreading flowers before the bride as she walks into the *mandap* creates a delightful spectacle. Flower girls and ring bearers should be least four years old to appreciate the significance of the ceremony.

Center pieces and Decorations:

Use your imagination to come up with center pieces that match the mood and style of the wedding. Fresh flowers, candle holders, *divi* (a holder for the oil lamp) – anything goes as long as it sets the right tone for your guests. Keep in mind the height of the piece since your guests will be talking over it and if it is too tall then it may become a hindrance.

Transportation

Avoid wearing anything black in your wedding since black is considered an inauspicious color for wedding.

Transportation is one of the most crucial element of any wed-

66

ding planning. Transportation for the bride and the groom and his party as well as all the out-of-town guests. Any confusion creates logistical problems, and can ruin the day for those affected.

As soon as you receive all your RSVPs, go over the guest list to see how many will be arriving from out of town. Some guests may need to be picked up at the airport, driven to the parties, transported to the ceremony, and then taken back to the airport or hotel the for the night. Find out their travel plans as soon as possible – their flight time, number, from where is the flight arriving – and allow time for delays. Let them know who is picking them up and that person's phone number. Tell them where will they be met and other arrangements.

Transportation also includes the *vara yatra (barat)*. How will the bride be taken to the wedding hall? Who is driving her? In which car? These are small details but attention to them is vital to make your wedding enjoyable for everyone.

For your guests arriving by car, check that there is enough parking at the wedding venue. Are other functions happening at the same time? If so, will parking be a problem? Find out these details when you look into the hall.

The Reception:

Your reception is a marvelous opportunity to create an integrated mix of Western and Eastern cultures. However, you need to be careful not to lose those aspects of each culture you are trying to capture. Choose carefully; think about what enhances your wedding and the kind of guests you are expecting.

Consider the following:

Assign an usher who can seat elderly relatives before the rest of the guests.

If you have children at your reception – more likely than not – provide a room with toys and games.

The kind of music your guests may enjoy, particularly if you have different age groups attending your wedding.

The dietary needs of your guests. Does your wedding happen to fall on *ekadashi* (a special day of fasting). If so, some of your guests may want special food.

Head table:

Many Indian weddings in America have incorporated the custom of having a head table for the newly-weds and their immediate families (often including grandparents and siblings).

You want to create a sense of balance for both families. A crowded head table takes away the significance of the couple, so use your judgment.

Wedding Cakes:

Although not traditional, having a wedding cake is being included in many Indian weddings. Be sure to discuss this with both families.

Bride and Groom cutting cake

If you decide to have one, start selecting a cake three months before your wedding, either from your caterer or a specialist baker. Set a budget.

The traditional three-tiered cake serves about 70 guests. With your supplier, decide details such as filling, icing and cake top. Make sure you and the supplier are clear about the number of servings, the date, time, delivery and location. Create an individual design that reflects your marriage. Display your cake prominently at the reception. Think of the timing for serving – you do not want to serve it immediately after the entree. The ideal time may be towards the end of the evening, but not so late so that some guests may have left.

How to Cut a Cake

Keep bride's right hand on the handle of a sharp knife with the groom's hand over the bride's hand.. Cut to the bottom of the cake with the point of the blade and then remove a slice. Serve each other a tiny piece and then offer it to your parents. After that the caterer or someone else in the family should take over and offer it to guests.

Pooja Accessories:

In a Hindu wedding, each ceremony calls for accessories such as *kumkum*, a coconut and fresh flowers. Discuss with your priest what is needed at least a month in advance and make a list. (Many priests bring their own *pooja* accessories.) Check with him the quantities and times when he will need them. For example, if you are taking the *vara yatra (barat)* from your house, you will need some items when you leave and others when you return with the bride. Make sure you have sufficient quantities. Put them in separate packages – this will eliminate confusion and delay during the ceremony. Keep the *pooja* accessories in a large plate They look attractive and are easily available during the ceremony. Prepare the *thal* (plate) a few days before the wedding.

Keep Pooja accessories ready in a plate for each ceremony.

Assign a team of people to help manage transportation for your guests.

Suggested List of Pooja and other Accessories

Plain or decorated coconut

4 wooden sticks (small) 2, *kodia* (divi), thread

Aarti plate with *diya, kumkum,* colored rice

2 fresh flower garlands

Sri Ganesh idol (small) or coin

Ten *suparies* (bettle nuts) for *navargaha* and Ganesh

Fresh flowers

Kumkum power and *haldi* powder

Agarbati (incense)

Ghanti (bell)

Colored rice grains for blessing

4 plates, 4 bowls, and 6 spoons

Kalash with water

Puffed rice or *Daanger* or *Jav* to offer in *Agni*

HomaKunda

Ghee for offering in *Agni*

Match box

Small pieces of Duraflame log for *Agni Homa*

Small wooden sticks if the *pooja* is outdoors

A pedestal fan to circulate air

Small kitchen fire extinguisher for emergency

Bowl containing sweets for *prasad*

Shawl or silk cloth of Beige color to be used as *antarpat*

A silver coin for *hastmilap*

Red thread to tie on the wrists of the couple (*mindhal*)

Mangalsutra

Dupatta for bride and *Upvastra* for groom

Coconut for breaking at the *vidai* time

Small table to place *Homa Kunda a*nd other items

Program hand-outs

Shahnai tape or CD

Clip-on microphone for the priest

Bajat (small footstool)   (Courtesy: Shri Jayant Sane)

Music and Entertainment:

In a Hindu wedding, music has a special place and each event can be enhanced through music. For example, on the night before the wedding, folk songs and dances can make for a lively and enjoyable atmosphere. During the wedding ceremony, ask some family members to sing traditional wedding songs (*lagna geet*) – they will create a very special mood.

A Word of Caution:

When selecting the music, pay special attention to the words. Make sure you are comfortable with the meaning – explicit and implicit – of each song.

For the reception, select the best music group you can. Talk to them several times, and, if possible, watch them play. Find out exactly what kind of music they are going to play and when. Not paying attention to such details can create a very embarrassing situation. Today, it is possible to have a live music played during your cocktail hour or any other time. Keep in mind that music can be the key in creating mood for your guests at your wedding.

Jewelry:

Jewelry occupies a prominent place in any Hindu wedding. It is not only woven with symbolism and tradition but it is also often considered her property, particularly the *chudo* (a bangle) and *mangalsutra*. Jewelry also indicates a family's status. *Mangalsutra* is an integral part of the Hindu marriage ethos and is often one of the most treasured pieces of jewelry in her collection.

Assign a person - a close friend or a family member - to coordinate events of the day

Interestingly, the tradition and style of *mangalsutra* goes back to the times of Mohenjodaro civilization or even earlier. In its original form, the *mangalsutra* or *kartha mani* is a chain of black beads with a gold disc-shaped pendant, however, the style of pendants vary in different parts of India.

Wedding Favors for Your Guests:

Although giving something to your guests as a token and as a way of thanking them is not an Indian custom, it has been incorporated into many marriages performed in America.

Select a gift that reflects your style and taste. You can choose something Indian – a silver *kankavati* (vermillion powder holder) or a pair of *dandia* (decorated sticks) – or something American – such as a ceramic basket filled with heart shaped cookies. Be creative in selecting and giving wedding favors for your guests. How about a nice package that includes your favorite quote?

Jewelry

Mehndi:

Mehndi designs on the bride's hands and feet have been part of weddings in India for generations.

Mehndi artists available in many areas. Look at the portfolio of your artist, and make sure that you feel comfortable with her style. Find out the cost, the time involved to apply it, and how long are you expected to keep the henna on. Allow yourself ample time to get the optimum color. Schedule the appointment well in advance.

For the application, prepare a comfortable setting with lots of pillows, paper towels, music, and friends to keep you company.

When choosing the color of your nail polish keep in mind that certain colors such as pink and magenta do not go well with *mehndi*. Dark, earthy colors go very well.

Take pictures when the *mehndi* is wet. They come out the best

Have someone ready with "bride-crisis kit", with extra stockings, anti-static cling spray, mirror, brush, safety pins, deodorant, lipstick, extra blush, tissues, a list of the wedding party's phone numbers and everyone you have hired.

Wear loose fitting clothes - especially pants - for applying the mehndi.

Computers and the Internet:

You may use computer technology and the Internet to organize your wedding, keep your guests informed, send invitations, and receive RSVPs. You need to be careful, however. For example, if you are planning a very formal wedding and send your invitations via email, it may not create the impression you want.

Here are some of the ways you can use your computer.

Desktop calendar: for planning and organizing.

Spread sheet: for budgeting and comparing costs

Database: for resources, guest lists, gift records.

Word processing: for correspondence with vendors.

Desktop publishing: for designing maps, directions, and other communications.

Web pages: for keeping friends and distant relatives up-to-date with information and sharing wedding pictures.

How Are You Related?

Who is Who at the Wedding

A wedding creates a whole set of new relationships and a brand new family. Interestingly, each new relationship has a special word in a Hindu family. For example, husband's younger brother is called *devar* but husband's older brother. is called *jyesth*. We find that this is very unique to a Hindu family and it is because the unit of a *parivar* (family) is at the heart of a Hindu life. Here we have given the sanskrit word for most major relationships. Please note that regional languages will have different words for each one of these relationships. It may be fun for you two to find out these words in your own language.

Vara : Groom

Vadhoo: Bride

Putrawadhoo: Daughter-in-law

Jamata (Damad): Son-in-law

Shyali (Saali): Bride's sister to the groom

Shyal: Bride's brother to the groom

Samdhi: Groom's parents to the bride's parents and bride's parents to the groom's parents

Devar: Groom's younger brother to the bride

Devarani: Devar's wife to the bride

Nanand: Groom's sister to the bride

*Nando*i: *Nanand*'s husband

Did you know that most of the words for family members such as Father, Mother, Brother, and sister come from Sanskrit?

75

Jyesth: Groom's older brother

*Jethan*i: Wife of the older brother of the groom

Shawsoor: Father-in-law

Shwashru: Mother-in-law

Bhabhi (Bhatrujaya): Brother's wife

Mama: Maternal uncle

Mami: Maternal aunt

Taoji: Father's older brother

Taiji: Father's older brother's wife

Chacha: Father's younger brother

Chachi: Father's younger brother's wife.

Dada: Grandfather

Dadi: Grandmother

Nana: Maternal grandfather

Nani: Maternal grandmother

Didi: Sister

Jijaji: Sister's husband

Legal Matters

Making it Official

Just as a marriage brings a whole set of new relatives, it also brings some legal and administrative matters that you need to take care of in order to make your transition into the new life easy. Here is a list of some of the things you need to do before you get married.

Blood Test

Depending upon the state in which you live, you may both need to take a blood test before you get your marriage license. Though this is an outdated test that was used to detect syphilis - a sexually transmitted decease - many states still require it before you get your license. The test only takes minutes, and the results are often back the next day. Most health insurance policies will cover pre-marital blood tests.

Marriage License

For your marriage to be legal, you need a marriage license. You both need to go to your local city or town hall and apply for the license. You will need your blood test results, and will be required to fill out an application. After a three-day waiting period, one of you can go and pick up the application which will be filled out by your priest. Send the completed application back to the

Changing names

This can be awkward. In previous times, a bride automatically changed her last name to her husband's. In many places she even changed her first name, though this was not common. You both need to discuss this issue. The final decision will depend on several factors and your choice should make you feel comfortable for the rest of your life.

If you decide to change your name you need to know how to do it. Start with large institutions and work your way down. First you want to change your name on your driver's license. Take a copy of your certified marriage license along with your present license. You will also need to change your name on your social security card. Call the local Social Security office and request a change of name application. They will need to see your certified marriage license. Follow the procedure with your bank accounts, credit cards, utilities and other documentation.

How to Be Successfully Married

Friendly Guidelines

1. Respect each other.

2. Show that you care.

3. Share higher ideals and uplifting thoughts with each other.

4. Take time out from your busy life for just each other.

5. Pursue your individual hobbies or activities.

6. Remember that it takes efforts to create a happy family.

7. Think more about what you can give to the relationship - not what you get.

8. Assign at least one part of the daily routine together - going for a walk, eating dinner, or listening to music.

9. Remember that any good relationship goes through ups and downs so learn to accept them as natural.

10. Trust each other.

Now That You Are Married

Welcome to Grihasthashrama

समानो मन्त्रः समितिः समानी
समानं मनः सह चित्तमेषाम् ।
समानं मन्त्रमभिमन्त्रये वः
समानेन वो हविषा जुहोमि ।।

Welcome to the life of a householder. Now that you are married, many things will change in your life - including your own views about life itself. Now you have entered one of the most responsible phase of your life. Your philosophy, your goals, your education, everything will come into play to make your life a wonderful experience and make you an important member of the community.

Since you have married in the Hindu tradition, you may be interested in finding out the Hindu view of life. According to Hindu philosophy, the human being is potentially divine and the goal of each one of us is to unfold that Divinity within us. By leading a righteous life, and following the Eternal and Universal Law of Creation - known as *Sanatana Dharma* - we can achieve this goal. There are four distinct stages of a human life described as *Chatur Ashram.*

First Stage: *Brahmacharya Ashram* (life of celibacy)

Each individual (I -consciousness) tries to excel in the field of knowledge, earns physical fitness and builds character. The goal in this stage of life is to equip oneself so that one may follow the path of *Dharma.*

Second Stage: *Grihasthashrma* (life of a householder)

The husband and wife (We -consciousness) nurture a happy family, excel in their profession, business or services, create wealth following the dictums of *Sanatana Dharma*, share love and care for all.

This state of life is considered the most difficult. Householders learn to expand their consciousness and become one with joys and sorrows of all family members. The goal of householder's life is to unfold human divinity through joint efforts of husband and wife.

Third Stage: *Vanprasthashram*

With the birth of grandchildren, householders try to cultivate collective consciousness. In this retirement stage, they learn to love all human beings and serve them. The goal of life here is to unfold divinity through social service.

Fourth Stage: *Sanyas Ashram*

In this stage of self-realization, one tries to cultivate universal consciousness. One learns to identify with the entire cosmos. The goal of life here is to unfold Divinity through unselfish love for God.

Making it a Home

Home is Where the Heart Is

Probably one of the first things your friends ask you is: " have you found a place to live yet?" Although traditionally in a Hindu family the newly married couple lived with the groom's family, today either due to a job or by personal choice most young couples choose to live on their own. So as soon as you get married you want to set-up your place of living - your castle. Since you probably have a very good idea about what you will need to start your life - a living room suite, a bed, kitchen accessories, a dining table and so forth, we have not included the list of those items here. We also know that the furniture and the kitchen accessories are of such a personal choice that you do not need any guidelines or assistance. However, since you have chosen to get married by a *Vedic* ceremony, we believe that you may be interested in creating a home that reflects your values. Here are some suggestions to help you get started on that end.

Shrine

We recommend that you assign a small corner in your new home - either in your kitchen, your spare bedroom or your bedroom for a small shrine. It is easy. All you need is a picture or a statue of a deity, an incense holder, and a small *divi* for lighting a *diya* (lamp) every morning. In most Hindu homes lighting a *diya* and offering a small prayer at this shrine is part of a morning routine.

Kitchen

If you want to cook Indian meals - regularly or occasionally - you will need some special spices and herbs.

When entertaining guests in your new home, try playing Indian classical music in the background. It will add clasical touch to your entertaining.

Here is a list of most used spices and herbs that you will be able to buy from an Indian or health food grocery store. Stock up your kitchen with these essentials.

Spices

Haldi powder

Jeera powder

Chili powder

mustard seeds

Garam masala

Curry powder

Chat masala

Kitchen Accessories

Rolling Pin

Pressure Cooker

Blender

Food Processor

Furniture

Although not practical for everyone, a *jhoola* (swing) also adds Indian touch to your home. If you like the idea but are going to rent an apartment, you may want to consider a self-standing *jhoola*.

Other decorating tips

Select pictures and other decorations carefully to create the kind of environment you two want.

Remember that sights, sounds, and fragrance together can create wonders in your home that is uniquely yours..

List of important vendors

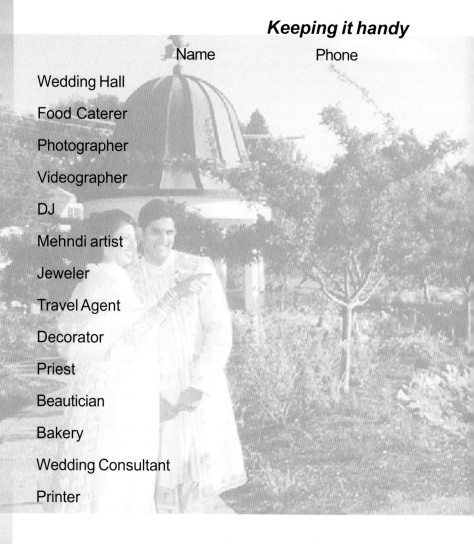

Keeping it handy

	Name	Phone
Wedding Hall		
Food Caterer		
Photographer		
Videographer		
DJ		
Mehndi artist		
Jeweler		
Travel Agent		
Decorator		
Priest		
Beautician		
Bakery		
Wedding Consultant		
Printer		

Creating Sweet Memories

Highlights of our wedding

Resources

Resources

Your Most Important Ally

No matter how good the planning, your entire wedding day is in the hands of your vendors. Your beautician, hall decorator, food caterer, photographer and DJ can make or break your day. That is why it is important that you choose each one of them carefully and only after checking out their references. Here is a list of resources - from food caterers to hall decorators - to help you start your search. This list is by no means comprehensive. Please keep in mind that although we have tried our best to make sure that all our resources are current, the entire industry is in the constant state of evolution. Also, many service providers operate from their homes, making it difficult to track their address or phone changes. We hope that this list helps you find the services in your area or at least it will give you a starting point for your search.

Note: If you find these resources helpful, please tell them that you found them here. In addition, if you find new resources that are useful, please send them to us so that we can add in our next edition. Thanks and Good Luck.

Flowers

Asian Flower
921 North Rodgers
Irving, Texas 75601
800-622-8229

Fresh Flower Garlands
P.O.Box 11213
New Brunswick, NJ 08906
732 –248-9424

Unique Flowers and Gifts
2940 W. Lincoln Ave., #B
Anaheim, CA 92801
714-527-5322
310-929-4749

Wedding Consutlants

Mandap
Anuradha Patel
Lata Patel
133 Northfield Road
Parsippany, NJ 07054
973-884-1355
973-334-5479

Mangalam
Shishir Sheth
614 Buckingham Drive
Piscataway, NJ 08854
732-463-7888
732-463-8081 (Fax)

Majestic Celebration
Meenal Patel
30658 Chimney Lane
Union City, CA 64587
510-471-4648
909-279-4030

All Wedding Services
Shamsha Daria
94-30 6th Ave
Apt 3G
Elmhurst, NY 11373
718-699-3170

Avsar
Sandhya Patel/ Kalpana Patel
1692 Oak Tree Road
Sugar Tree Plaza
Edison, NJ 08820
732 603-0636

Utsav Decorations
Krishna Mistry
1340 Stelton Road
Piscataway, NJ 08854
732-777-2140

Nalini Creations
Wedding and Events Planner
46 Anselm Way
Sudbury, MA 01776
978-579-9732

Vivah Fashions Accessories
220 Yonge Street
Toronto Eaton Center
Toronto ON MJB2H1
Canada
416 598 3415

Regency Wedding Services
1 888 746 3667

Abhishek
1039 Green Street
Iselin NJ 08830
732 283 2565

Elegant Affairs
6 Apache Way
Montville, NJ 07045
973 334 7340

California Weddings
Exclusive contract with 28 hotels
Frances Farzanch
1508 Grand
Santa Anna CA 92705
949 448 1857 phone
949 415 0759 fax

Wedding Invitations

Sir Speedy Printing
2960 W. Lincoln Ave.
Anaheim, CA 92801
714-527-3122
714-527-6585 (Fax)

Bhagyoday Printers
91 Princeton Garden
Piscataway, NJ 08854
908-968-3653

Advanced Graphic Services
Aruna Shah
1460 SW 3rd Street
Pompano Beach, FL 33069
954-784-8100
954-784-8101 (Fax)
www.deshvidesh.com/wedding.html

Printing and Graphic Services
For Creative Printing Solutions
Neelam Wali
505 Middlesex Turnpike # 8
Billerica, MA 01821
978 667 6950
978 667 5167 (Fax)
email awali@gis.net
www.gis.net~wali/print.html

Devotional and Wedding items

Pooja International
34159 Freemont Blvd.
Freemont, CA 94555
510-793-7930
510-793-7026 (Fax)

Food Catering

Chawpatty Restaurant and Catering Service
1349-1351 Oak Tree Road
Iselin, NJ 008830
908-283-9020
908-283-9030 (Fax)

Rangoli
Koki Shah
825 Rte 1 South
Iselin, NJ 08830
908-855-1177

Sukhadia's Sweets 'n' snacks
1677 Oak Tree Road
Edison, NJ 08820
732-548-1888

Banana Leaf Indian Restaurant
3737 W. Lawrence Ave.
Chicago, IL 60625
312-539-7315

Candlelight International
466 Hempstead Turnpike
Elmont NY 11003
516 328 1531

Viceroy of India
19W 555 Roosevelt Road
Lombard, IL 60148
630-627-4411
and
2520 W.Devon Ave
Chicago, IL 60659
312-743-4100

Cuisine of India
2348 S. Elmhurst Road
Mt.Prospect, IL 60056
847-718-1522
847-718-1523 (Fax)

Mayura Restaurant
1546 Ogden Ave.
Downers Grove, IL 60515
630-969-3696

Peacock India Restaurant and Bar
701 North Milwaukee Ave.
#284 Rivertree Plaza
Vernon Hills, IL 60061
847-816-3100

Shehnai Cuisine of India
705 E. Birch Street
Suite P
Brea, CA 92621
714-990-8989
714-990-8990 (Fax)

India House Restaurant
Contact: Mukesh
7775 Beach Blvd.
Buena Park, CA 90620
714-670-2114
714-670-0510 (Fax)

Taj of India
1356 W. Valley Parkway
Suite D
Escondido, CA 92029

Chiraag
Cuisine of India
2701, 190th Street
Redondo Beach, CA 90278
310-370-1097 (call Balbir)

Uphaar
Mahesh Savali
908-283-2802
908-636-2910

Angithi
2047 E. Fowler Ave.
Tampa, FL [AU: zip code?]
813-979-4889

Videography & Photography

Shivani Productions
Jay Patel
11-13 Central Main Ave.
Passaic, NJ 07055
201-338-9337 (Home)
201-779-1913 (Business)

Creative Channel
847-299-0429

Global Photography
Yogesh Patel
7258 Pecan Avenue
Moor Park CA 93021
800-529-7557

A1 Photography and Video
15868 E. Imperial Hwy.
La Mirada, CA 90638
310-947-8540

Photowala, Anita
44861 Lynx Drive
Fremont, CA 94539
510-659-1057

Punjab Photography
726 Santa Rosa Street
Sunnyvale, CA 94086
408-737-0289

Wide Angle Photo & Video
973 340 7282

Jalaram Video Production and Entertainment
Janak Patel
9311 Voit's Lane
Philadelphia, PA 19115
215-934-7341

Ameecar Photo and Video
1405 Oak Tree Road
Iselin, NJ 08830
732 283 9898

Sumit Arya Photography
1 888 746 3667

Circle (K) Photo & Video
Thomas KallaDanthyil
954-437-3974

Video Creations
305-623-2937

Salsan International
4032 N.W. 9th Ave., (Powerline Road)
Ft. Lauderdale, FL 333309
954-561-8293

TEI Inc.
2216 N. Dixie Hwy.
Boca Raton, FL 33431
561-392-3506

Video Works
9725 Bissonnet # B3
Houston TX 77036

Asian Video
8019 Tamarron Dr
Plainsboro, NJ 08536
609 275 0995

LagnaGeet (Wedding Songs) & Music:

Smita Shah
362 Hadleigh Lane
North Brunswick, NJ 08902
908-422-4994
908-283-7077 (Fax)

Soundtrax Disc Jockey
973-857-7593
973-325-9402

E.Arts London Ltd.
Finest Dance Entertainment
310-281-6841

Fun time DJ
7 Rock Wood Lane
South Lawrence, NJ 01843
978-682-2701

Yamin & The Patel's Orchestra
561-640-4031 (Yamin Patel)
561-967-8537 (Muzammil Patel)

Khayaal, Atif Sakrani
305-667-5463

Teji's Entertainment
908 422 7572

Yamin and The Patel's Orchestra
561 640 4031 (Yamin Patel)
561 967 8537 (Muzammil Patel)

Khayaal
Atif Sakrani
305 667 5463

Priests and Pundits

Pandit Mohanlal
6 Covert Avenue
New Hyde Park, NY 11040
516-354-0299
516-616-6174 (Fax)

Jayant Sane
32 Pamila Road
Framingham MA 01701
508 877 5498

Wedding Halls

The Olympic Collection
11301 Olympia Blvd
West Los Angeles, CA
310 575 4585

Shahnawaz Restaurant and Banquet Hall
5634 E. LaPalma Ave
Anaheim Hills, CA 92807
818 265 0666

New Delhi Palace (Restaurant and hall)
119 South Brand Blvd.
Glendale, CA 91204
818-265-0666

Cafe Bombay
4546 El Camino Real, #5
Village Court Shopping Center
Los Altos, CA 94022
415-948-9463

Sneha
1214 Apollo Way, Suite 404
Sunnyvale, CA 94086
408-736-2720

Uphaar
Mahesh Savali
908-283-2802
908-636-2910

Pasand (Three branches)
3701 El Camino Real
Santa Clara, CA
408-241-5150

Pasand
2286 Shattuck Ave.
Berkeley, CA
510-549-2559

Pasand
802 B Street
(Downtown off 101)
San Rafael, CA
415- 456-6099

The Cotillion
"The Wedding Place"
4400 Jericho Tpke. (Rt 25)
Jericho, NY
516-938-3300

California Weddings
Exclusive arrangement with 28 hall
Frances Farzanch
1508 Grand
Santa Anna CA 92705
949 448 1857 phone
949 415 0759 fax

Horoscope Matching Service

New Dynamic Inc.
800-NEW-DYNA
707-869-1763
nick@newdyna.com

Vedic Astrology, Pujas and Fire
Ceremonies by Pundit Pravin Jani
PO Box 13866
Berkeley, CA 94712-4866
510-843-0212
510-655-3382 (Fax)

Stephen Quong (Umananda)
17513 Grizzly Den Road
Lake Shastina, CA 96094
916-938-2997
umananda@aol.com
www.jyotisha.com

Chhabil Patel
1340 Merrimac Lane
Hanover Park, IL 60103
630-213-0144

Arvind Desai
423 7th Street, Apt 206
Moti Mahal Restaurant
2525 W.Devon Ave.
Chicago, IL 60659
312-262-2080
312-262-2081

Astro Genetic Vision
Dr. V Sahni
22201 Sherman Way
Canoga Park, CA 91303
818-346-5697
818-346-6593 (Fax)

Dr. Vishnu Sharma
94-30 6oth Ave., 4C
Elmhurst, NY 11373
718-699-6414

94

Jewelers:

Jain Jewelers
Nilima Jain
1352 Oak Tree Road
Iselin, NJ 08830

Shingar Jewelers
7208 W. Oakland Park Blvd.
Ft. Lauderdale, FL 33313
954-749-4339

Alpha Omega Jewelers
Harvard Square
57 JFK Street
Cambridge, MA
800-447-4367

Chennikkara Jewelers
7412 Janes Ave.
Woodridge, IL 60515
630-960-9100
630-960-9109
630-960-9125 (Fax)

Laxmi Jewelers
2617 W. Devon Ave.
Chicago, IL 60659
312-764-2790
312-764-2799 (Fax)

Silver Arts Jewelers
2721 W. Devon Ave.
Chicago, IL 60659
312-465-2466
312-465-2467 (Fax)

Silvex Jewelers
736 East Schaumburg Road
Schaumburg, IL 60194
847-310-4633
847-310-8677 (Fax)

Meghana Jewelers
885 East Schaumburg Road
Schaumburg, IL 60194
847-895-1010
847-895-1011 (Fax)

Gold Palace Jewelers
1085 University Ave.
Berkeley, CA 94710
510-848-5050

Krishna Jewelers
18435 South Pioneer Blvd.
Artesia, CA 90701
310-402-7662
310-809-7662
310-924-5711 (Fax)

Vitha Jewelers Inc.
18501 Pioneer Blvd.
Artesia, CA 90701
310-402-4641
310-402-3812

Highglow
18618 Pioneer Blvd.
Artesia, CA 90701
310-402-0112
URL: http://www.highglow.com

Sonya Pearls and Corals
18528 S.Pioneer Blvd., Suite 204
Bhindi Plaza
Artesia, CA 90701
310-924-7665

Jaipur Jewelers
20/22 Marconi Ave.
Iselin, NJ 08830
908-283-9615
908-283-9616

Bhindi Jewelers (Los Angeles)
18508 Pioneer Blvd.
Artesia, CA 90701
562-402-8755

Bhindi Jewelers (Atlanta)
1070 Oak Tree Road
Decatur, GA 30033
404-325-8755

Bhindi Jewelers (San Francisco)
5970 Mowry Ave.
Newark, CA 94560
510-797-8755

Vaibhav Jewelers
1209 U.S. Hwy. 17-92 South
Longwood, Florida 32750
407-696-0034

Babylon Jewelry
3630 N. State Rd. 7
Lauderdale Lakes, FL 33319
954-735-1384

Bombay Jewelry Company
34143 Fremont Blvd.
Fremont, CA 94555
510-745-0993

Zevar Jewelers
6344 W. Oakland Park Blvd.
(Inverrama Plaza)
Sunrise, FL 33313
954-742-5305

Shingar Jewelers
7208 W. Oakland Park Blvd.
Ft Lauderdale, FL 33313
954-749-4339

Beauty and Bridal Needs:

Amrita Udeshi
508-875-8348

Mehndi
Jayshree Nensey
661 S. Calvados Ave.
Covina, CA 91723
626-332-8843

**Salon a Rivaz
Beauty Services**
679 N. Cass Ave.
Westmont, IL 60559
630-323-8555

Usha Beauty Salon
(Specialist in Indian bridal make-up and *mehndi*)
7712-B Harford Road
Baltimore, MD 21234
410-661-8204 (office)
410-665-2255 (home)

Shaz
24 W.445 Lake Street
K-Plaza
Roselle, IL
630-894-8883

Aanchals Beauty Services
18622 Pioneer Blvd.
Artesia, CA 90701
310-809-1646

Suman
703-493-1046
703 690 4919
for pre-wedding ceremonies with
mehndi artists and beauticians

Amita Mehta
Mehndi Design
Norwood, MA
617 255 5877

Rashmi Jhaveri
Bridal make-up and mehndi design
732 283 0899

Wedding Cakes:

Neena Vaswani
755 River Road
Teaneck, NJ 07666
For custom-made Indian style
wedding cakes.

Clothing:

Bourjois Clothing
2750 West Devon Ave.,
Chicago Ill 60659
773 262 4722

Khazana Boutique
659 N.Cass Ave.,
Westmont Ill 60559
630 655 2220

Mona's Fashions
2706 W. Oakland Park Blvd
Ft. Lauderdale, FL
954 730 0098

Mem-Sahib
18185 Pioneer Blvd
Artesia CA 90701
310 402 7177

Sari Palace
1000 University Ave.,
Berkeley CA 94710
510 841 7274
510 841 4653

Kiran Saree Palace
1551 Oak Tree Road
Iselin NJ 08830

India Sari Palace
37-07 74th street
Jackson Heights, NY 11372
718 426 2700

Roopkala Plaza
5107 Western Blvd
Raleigh, NC 27606
919 851 1111

Bombay Sari Palace
11301 Orange Blossom Trail
Suite 201
Orlando FL 32837
407 856 1974

Libas Boutique
6350 W.Oakland Park Blvd
Sunrise, FL 33313
954 741 0894

Usha Boutique
10091 Sunset Strip
Fort Lauderdale, FL 33322
954 747 6664
954 394 7577

Chunari Collection
120 Coolidge Farm Road
Boxboro, MA 01719
978 263 5974

Sample Manglashtak (Gujarati)

સિદ્દિવ્ય બુદ્દિવ્ય પતિ રુડા ગણપતિ બ્રહ્મા શિવશંકર
લક્ષ્મી વિષ્ણુ સર્વ મુનિઋષિ યક્ષ અને કિન્નર
તેત્રીસ કોટિ દેવયોનિમાં જેને પિતૃઓ સર્વ તે
આવી આ શુભ સ્થળે વરવધૂ લગ્ન વદો મંગલે।

દેવો અપૉ દિવ્યતા દયા પ્રેમ દાને સદા રાખજો
માતાના વાત્સલ્યને પ્રીતિમાં સદા રાખજો
શાંતિ સંપતિમાં દંપતી સુખ સૈા દાખજો
સુકમૉ કરે મણે યશ દ્દનો થાય સદા મંગલમ્।।

આનંદમા રહીને જિંદગી શોભાવજો સુકમૅથી
બન્ને કુળનો આબરુમાં સામ્યતા સદા રાખજો
તારું મારું ભુલી તમે અન્યોન્યમાં પ્રીતિ વધારજો
શાંતિ કાંતિ સૌજન્યમાં થાય સદા મંગલમ્।

વિશ્વે કુટુંબભાવના રાખી દામ્પત્ય દીપાવજો
સર્વકલ્યાણ ભાવનામા ભાગ રુડો ભજવજો
વધે કીર્તિ મણે સફળતા કાર્યે આવા કરજો
એવી આશિષ ઑપીએ થાય સદા મંગલમ

દીપક તણા પ્રકાશની જ્યોત જેવી જગજગી
પ્રેરણા એ અર્પતી નવયુગલને ઈશારો કરી
અજ્ઞાનતાને દૂર કરી જ્ઞાનમાં લંડા ઉતરજો
પરોપકારના કાર્યેથી થાય સદા મંગલમ્।

મળો રિદ્દિ અને સિદ્દિ ગણપતિ ગણનાયક
સર્વદેવો લગ્ન મંડપે અહીં વિહરજો
વિહરતાં નવદંપતી પર પુષ્પવૃષ્ટિ કરજો
સ્વાગત આપનું કરતાં થાય સદા મંગલમ

થાય વૃદ્દિ કીર્તિની પ્રસન્નતા મણે લક્ષ્મી તણી
સિદ્દિ બુદ્દિ અને રિદ્દિ મળો શિવપુફત્ર ગણેશની
ઉત્સાહ અને ઉમંગમા મણે પ્રસન્નતા ભરી પૂરી
સન્માર્ગે સદા વિચરે તો થાય સદા મંગલમ

લગ્ન એતો જિવન તણુ માધ્યમ વંશ વૃદ્દિનું
ક્ષતિઓ એમાં થાય તો ભુલ કોની માનવીઋ
પવિત્રતા સંસ્કારિતા ને જોખમમાં મૂકશો નહીં
માનવી માનવ થાય તો થાય સદા મંગલમ

।। ઈતિ લગ્ન માંગલ્યે મંગલાષ્ટક સમાપ્ત ।।

Courtsey LagnaMangalya

Sample Manglashtak (Sanskrit)

यावच्छंकर मौलिगा सुग्नदीगौरी तद् अर्धांगना
यावत् प्रेमवती पयोब्धितनया यावद्धीनेशः गशिः ।
यावद्धेद पुराएशास्त्र महिमा यावच्य विप्णुस्थिति ।
स्तावत्त्वं धनधान्य संतति ह्युतो कुर्यात् सदा मंगलम् ।।

नित्योनित्य निरंजनो नर वरे नारायएो नारदो
नक्षत्राएि नभो नुसिंह नगरो नागाननो पन्नगः ।
नागेन्द्री नरवाहनो नरपति नीलानदी नर्मदा
नारीएाम् नयनाभिरामनिधाय कुर्यात् सदा मंगलम् ।।

आदित्या प्रमुखाश्व ये दिविचरा स्तारागएा चन्द्'मा
मेपाद्या अ अपिराशयो गएपति ब'हमेश लक्ष्मीधरा ।
खिल मातारोष्ट बसवः शकश्व सप्तपयँ
ते रक्षन्तु युवासदेव सगएाँ कुर्यात् सदा मंगलम् ।।

विघ्न ध्वान्त निवारएँक ताएि विंघ्नाटविहेव्यवाद्
विघ्न व्याल कुलाभिमान गरुडो विघ्नेभपंचानन ।
विघ्नो तुंग गिरि प्रभेदन पटु विघ्नझ्वुधौ वाडवो
विघ्नाधौध घन प्रचंड पवनो विघ्नेश्वरः कुर्यात् सदा मंगलम् ।।

गंगा सिन्धु सरस्वति च यमुना गोदावरी नर्मदा
कावेरी सरयु महेन्द्र तनया चर्मएवति वेदिका ।
क्षिप्रा वेगवती महासुर नदी ख्याता गया गंडकी
पूर्एा पूर्एाजलै समुद्र सहिताः कुर्यात् सदा मंगलम् ।।

लक्ष्मीः कौस्तुभ पारिजातक सुरा घन्वन्तरिश्चन्द्रमा
गावः कामदुघा सुरेश्वगजो रंभादि देवांगनाः ।
अश्वः सप्तमुखः सुघा हरिधनु शंखो विष चांबुजे
रत्नानीति चतुर्दशः प्रतिदिनं कुर्यात् सदा मंगलम् ।।

गंगा गोमति गोपति गएपति गोविंद गोवर्धनो
गीता गौत्रऽपि गोरजो गिरिसुता गंगाघरो गौतमः ।
गायत्री गरुडो गदा गिरि गुहा गंभीर गौदावरी
गंधर्वग्रह गोप गोकुलजना कुर्यात् सदा मंगलम् ।।

वाल्मीकिः सनकः सनातन तरुर्व्यासो वशिष्ठो भृगु
जाँवालिर्जदमदिग्न कच्छ जनको गर्गो गिरा गौतम् ।
मांघाता ऋतुपर्एवेन सगरा घन्यो दिलीपो नलः
पुएयो घर्मसुतो ययातिन न्हुपो कुर्वतु वो मंगलम् ।।

Courtsey LagnaMangalya

Glossary

Definitions of Key Words

In this book we have used many Sanskrit, Hindi, and various regional language words. Although we have tried to give their literal meanings here, please keep in mind that many of these words represent concepts that are not easily understood by the people who are not familiar with the culture or the religion. So please note that these meanings are only for you to understand the ceremony a little better. However, their true and in-depth meaning could only be understood in the total context in which they are used in the ceremony and elsewhere.

Adhibhauatic = material, physical world
Adhidaivik = non-physical world
Adhyatmic = spiritual world
Arati = a plate carrying lighted lamp used to greet groom
Agni = fire
Ahankar = the concept of individual ego identity
Akshat = grain of rice
Anand Karaj = ceremony of bliss
Adas = a reading from the holy book of Sikhs
Arundhati = seventh star of the constellation Great Dipper
Ashirvada = blessing
Ashram = *stage in life or a place of learning.*
Bahu = daughter-in-law
Bandha = suit
Bandhana = bondage
Barat = groom's procession
Barnu Rokvu = stopping at the door
Bhabhi (Bhatrujaya) = Brother's wife
Bhangra = folk dance from northern part of India
Bharai = to fill
Bidai/Vidai = farewell
Brahmacharya = celibacy
Burfee = a kind of sweet
Chacha = Father's younger brother
Chachi = Father's younger brother's wife.
Chandan = fragrant wood often used in worship

Chudo = bangle
Churha = bangle
Churidar = tight pajama
Dadi = grandmother
Damaad = son in law
Dan = donation
Danarpana = giving of wealth
Dandia = a pair of wooden sticks used in a folk dance
Darshan = sight
Deva = Deity
Devar = Groom's younger brother to the bride
Devarani= Devar's wife to the bride
Devagoon = ceremony
Devashastra =God's literature
Dharma = duty
Dharna = part of mangalya ceremony
Dhurvadarshan = looking at the polar star
Divi = oil-lamp holder
Doli = a special cart to carry the bride
Ekadash = eleventh day of the lunar calendar
Ganpathi/Ganesh = The Deity of Leadership and Auspiciousness
Garba = a folk dance from Gujarat
Gotras = ancestors
Gotrocchhara = taking the names of your ancestors
Grahashanti = peace for the planets
Gruhashanti = peace for the home
Grahastha = householder
Granth = a holy book
Gujarati = language spoken by people from the state of gujarat
Guru = teacher
Haldi = turmeric powder
Havan = a special pot for lighting fire
Havan kund = a place of sacrificial fire
Homa = offerings to the sacrificial fire
Indra = Lord of heaven
Isana = north-east direction
Ishtadevata = family deity
Jamata = son in law
Jaymala = victory necklace usually made of fresh flowers
Jethani= wife of the older brother of the groom
Jina-grahe-danarpana = giving of wealth at temple
Jyesth(Jeth) = Groom's older brother
Kangana = bangles
Kankavati = a small holder for vermillion
Kansar = whole wheat sweet
Kanyadan = giving away of the bride by her parents
Karaj = debt
Kashi = the city of Banares

Kubera = Treasurer of the Gods
Kuldevta = family deity
kumkum = a red vermilion powder used for the ceremony
Kunda = a small vessel
Lagna geet = traditional wedding songs
Laxmi = goddess of wealth
Lehenga = bridal dress
Livun = house cleaning
Ma = mother
Mami = bride's maternal aunt
Mang = parting of the hair
Madhuparka = giving of honey
Maharashtra = State in India
Mandap = canopy
Mangalfera = going around the fire by the couple
Mangalya = type of ceremony
Manglashtak = eight auspicious verses recited for the couple
Mangalsutra = a necklace offered by the groom to the bride
Marathi = people from Maharashtra
Mehandirat =night of henna design
Mehndi = henna
Milni =meeting
Muhurt = auspicious time
Nana = maternal grandfather
Nanand = Groom's sister to the bride
Nandoi = Nanand's husband
Nani = maternal grandmother
Narayana = Lord Vishnu
Panigrahan = taking of the hands of the bride by the groom as a token of getting married
Panetar = white sari with red design usually worn by the bride at the time of the wedding
Paraspara-mukha-avalokana = seeing each other's face
Parvati = Goddess - wife of Lord Shiva
Pithi = a paste made from turmeric powder
Pooja = ceremonial worship
Pooshi puza = flower worship
Putravadhu = daughter in law
Prabha = divine light
Pradakshina = going around
Pradana = to give
Pratishtha = to establish
Pujan = worshiping
Purnahuti = conclusion
Ram = Reincarnation of Lord Vishnu
Rasam = custom or tradition
Sagan = auspicious time
Salwar-kameez = two piece dress worn by brides from some

parts of India

Sam = equal

Samdhi = Groom's and bride's parents to each other

Sangeet = music

Sanyas = renunciation

Saptapadi = seven vows

Saubhagyavati = woman whose husband is alive

Sehera = veil of flowers

Seherabandi = putting of the veil of flowers on the head of the groom

Shawsoor = Father-in-law

Sherwani = a kind of dress worn by the groom

Shubha = auspicious

Shwashru : Mother-in-law

Shyal = bride's brother to the groom

Sindur = mustard colored powder

Sita = Lord Ram's wife

Skambha = Pillar

Slokas = a meter of 32 syllables in 4 stanzas

Sumuhurtam = an auspicious time

Supari = beetle nut

Sva-graha-agamana = coming back to one's own house

Syali = bride's sister to groom

Taiji= Father's older brother's wife

Taoji= Father's older brother

Thal = Plate

Tilak = dot on the forehead

Toran = ornamental arch on an entrance

Tumbak naari = long necked drum

Vadhu = bride

Vadhupravesh = bringing the bride home

Vanprastha = middle age

Vara = groom

Vara-ghoda = groom's procession on the horse

Varamala = fresh flower necklace for the groom

Vara-pratijna = vows taken by the groom

Varuna = Lord of water

Varyatra = procession

Vasashepa = a ceremony of giving blessing by the Guru to the disciple

Vayamkar = "we" consciousness

Vayu = wind

Vedi = pyre

Vidhi = ceremony

Vivah = wedding

Yama =Lord of death

Yatra = procession

Yoog =the age of the Universe.

About us:

Our goal is to make the vast and beautiful culture of India available to our future generations.. We believe that our rich heritage is so vast and yet complex that unless proper tools are given, it can get lost either in superficial behavior or rituals. Through our books we strive to bring the subtle beauty and inherent strength of this culture to the practical level where it can live and breath everyday through practice with understanding..To that end, please let us know how we are doing. Your comments and suggestions are welcome.

Other MeeRa Publications Books:

Pick A Pretty Indian Name for Your Baby: Over six thousand names with their authentic meanings and tips on selecting names that are appropriate outside of India.
Price $19.95
Pages 260
ISBN:0-9635539-0-9

Here Comes Diwali: Fully illustrated four color children's book that looks at this most celebrated festival from a child's point of view as he or she goes through various activities to prepare for the holiday.
Price: $6.95
Pages 16
ISBN: 0-9635539-1-7

Please send your comments or suggestions to:

MeeRa Publications
P.O. Box 812129
Wellesley, MA 02482
781-235-7441
www.MeeraPublications.com